P9-DEU-106

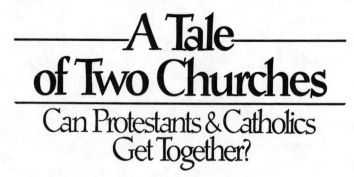

A Tale of Two Churches

Can Protestants & Catholics Get Together?

George Carey

**Foreword by
J. I. Packer**

INTERVARSITY PRESS
DOWNERS GROVE, ILLINOIS 60515

InterVarsity Press is the book-publishing division of Inter-Varsity Christian Fellowship, a student movement active on campus at hundreds of universities, colleges and schools of nursing. For information about local and regional activities, write IVCF, 233 Langdon St., Madison, WI 53703.

Distributed in Canada through InterVarsity Press, 860 Denison St., Unit 3, Markham, Ontario L3R 4H1, Canada.

Cover illustration: Jerry Tiritilli

ISBN 0-87784-972-2

Printed in the United States of America

Library of Congress Cataloging in Publication Data
Carey, George.
    A tale of two churches.

    Includes bibliographies.
        1. Protestant churches—Relations—Catholic Church.
    2. Catholic Church—Relations—Protestant churches.
    3. Evangelicalism.   I. Title.
    BX4818.3.C37   1985   280'.042   84-28858
    ISBN 0-87784-972-2

17	16	15	14	13	12	11	10	9	8	7	6	5	4	3	2	1
99	98	97	96	95	94	93	92	91	90	89	88	87	86	85		

112341

Foreword

Two days ago I heard that a Christian friend, middle-aged like me, was becoming a Roman Catholic. He is the second brilliant man I have known well to make this decision. Why have the two of them done this?

I think they turned to Roman Catholicism because, as biblically oriented Christians, they are aware of two things. First, they see that the church of Christ, that vast supernatural entity of which local churches are outcrops, is in itself one and that it is central to all God's plans for this world. Second, they see that human nature has been made for authority, that it is only fulfilled and contented when it is under authority, and that God is too good to leave his adopted children without definite authority to guide them. Knowing these things, they identify the one church with the Roman communion and the decisive authority with the Roman magisterium.

I applaud them for their two insights—which separate both their subjectivity and mine from any form of religious subjectivism, whether rationalist, pietist or mystical—but there I stop. I may be invincibly ignorant (heaven will show), but to me it seems clear that Scripture writers conceive (1) of a catholic visible church to which all believing and worshiping bodies, as such, belong, and (2) of the explicit teaching of the prophetic and apostolic Scriptures, brought home to us by the Holy Spirit, as our God-given authority. If they had been confronted with the idea of the church being infallible, I think they would have categorically denied it. So in the name of original, authentic Christianity I reject the two identifications that my friends make as mistaken. Nonetheless, I continue to think that those who are aware of the two things of which I spoke, and who have felt the pull of Rome in consequence, are better Christians at that point than those who have not.

George Carey focuses on the quest for theological accommodation that Vatican II encouraged and on the ground-level associations that charismatic renewal throughout the Christian world have produced. I am glad that he does, for I too have shared the pleasure and benefit of special-project and task-force cooperation with Roman Catholics on the basis of common loyalty to Scripture and to the Christ of Scripture, with interchurch questions temporarily shelved. Old Calvinist though I am, I have found working in Bible-based, Protestant-Catholic, charismatic-ecumenical networks for the faith of the creed and the vitality of the congregations to be an enriching experience that I would not have missed for the world, even though the charismatic worship style is not exactly, as we used to say in England, my cup of tea.

For myself I wish that Carey had said more about the currently urgent task of upholding faith in the Trinity, the Incarnation, the inerrancy of Scripture, and the primacy of the evangelistic and pastoral imperative according to Scripture, against the secularist, relativist and antinomian onslaughts to which these things are being subjected in our time both without and within the churches. I do not question that the painstaking pursuit of progress in fields of doctrinal adjustment is important. I have given time to it myself and may well do so again. But if I am any judge, the cobelligerence of Catholics and Protestants fighting together for the basics of the creed is nowadays more important, if only because until the cancerous spread of theological pluralism on both sides of the Reformation divide is stopped, any talk of our having achieved unity of faith will be so irrelevant to the real situation as to be both comic and pathetic. Comic because it will be so false, and pathetic because the unity formulas will at once be swallowed and relativized by the socio-secularist juggernaut ideology which is currently devouring the true, intended sense of formulas of faith in our separate circles of communion.

Nonetheless, the information that Carey provides is a necessary briefing for anyone who at any stage and at any level comes into the world of Catholic-Protestant identities and relationships, and the way he presents it is a model of good will. So it is a pleasure to commend his book to the Christian public.

J. I. Packer

Preface

This book had an interesting birth. James Hoover, associate editor
of InterVarsity Press, wrote to me asking if I would be interested
in writing a book about Protestant-Catholic relationships from an
evangelical perspective. What he did not know was that I had been
pondering at that very time what chance there was of doing exactly
that! So close was our thinking that this book is the outcome.

More than four centuries have passed since Western Christendom
split into Protestantism and Roman Catholicism. Many of the issues
that divided us then continue to raise their ugly heads, and, as old
stereotypes and deep emotions take hold, dialog often gives way to
polemics and attack. My hope is to suggest a way forward toward
genuine dialog and the resolution of conflict.

I will be misread if my attempts to show movement and progress
are seen as evidence that I do not believe that truth is important or
that I believe that the Reformation issues no longer matter. The
Reformation issues remain the major obstacles to any real unity

between Roman Catholic and Protestant Christians. Regrettably, we have not solved all the problems which surround Mary and the saints, faith and works, tradition and biblical authority, the church and sacraments. But, I will argue, neither do we still live in the sixteenth century. Things have changed within both Catholicism and Protestantism.

In this regard I think it is especially important that Protestants learn to recognize that real changes can take place in Roman Catholic theology without there ever being any official repudiation of past positions. It is simply part of the fabric of Roman Catholic theology to reinterpret the faith as time goes by, laying stress in new areas and de-emphasizing old ideas without announcing the changes. This is perhaps a very un-Protestant thing to do, but Protestants are bound to misunderstand current Roman Catholic thinking if they do not recognize this phenomenon.

I must confess that I am an optimist. I have high hopes not only for an increase in mutual understanding but also for the eventual reunion of the two streams of Western Christendom. Nevertheless, I hope I am a realist as well, and perhaps a few words of caution are in order.

First, I am not arguing for unity at the expense of truth. Unity, if it is to be biblical, must be unity in spirit and in truth.

Second, the Catholicism I describe here is largely that of Great Britain and the United States. No doubt, the accommodation with indigenous religions that takes place in Latin America, Africa and Asia is an issue which ought to be thought through in a larger context. But for the purposes of this book I have felt it more important that we learn to love and understand the neighbors whom we can see rather than those we cannot.

Third, as is certainly true of Protestants, not all Catholics agree. While to show change I refer to many Catholic theologians who seem to be moving in a Protestant direction, I know there are those who resist change. Nevertheless, the theologians I discuss are not atypical of Roman Catholic thought. They are very influential, even those who have stirred up controversy and aroused suspicion.

Moreover, I have not quoted controversial theologians on particularly controversial subjects. I have quoted them in areas where they represent a major current in Roman Catholic thought.

Fourth, I realize that many readers may not accept my thesis that a reunion of divided Christendom is desirable. Isn't the spiritual unity of true believers, they will ask, all that really counts? My answer is that that will do for a start. But is it not desirable that such spiritual unity be incarnated in structures that reflect it? I think the burden of proof lies with those who believe spiritual unity is enough. For eleven centuries, until the division between East and West, there was only one church, whatever diversities lay within it. There seems no reason in principle that it should not be so again.

Fifth, I hope that as well as helping evangelicals to appreciate the insights of Catholics this book will help Catholics to understand that the evangelical position does not proceed from a bigoted and arrogant standpoint but from a Christ-centered faith that yearns for a biblically based unity.

Finally, I have not written for theological pundits but for average Christians. To assist this purpose I have drawn from my recent pastoral experience at St. Nicholas' Church, Durham, to illustrate many of my points. In fact, the primary imagery of the chapter titles is drawn from the regions where I have worked. In a famous beauty spot near Barnard Castle, the dark and often wild River Greta joins the more peaceful River Tees to make it stronger and deeper. This "Meeting of the Waters" has been made famous through the painting by Joseph Mallard Turner and the poem "Rokeby" by Sir Walter Scott. For my purposes, this imagery expresses my hope that the waters of the two great Western church traditions may one day meet in spirit and in truth.

I must thank a number of friends who have assisted me in innumerable ways. Pride of place must go to Eileen, my wife, for being the friend and support she always is, and also to my long-suffering family. I am grateful to the Reverend David Gillett of the Christian Renewal Centre and to Mrs. Alison Moore of St. Nicholas', Durham, for the helpful criticisms they have made. Then there are those who have given me much help in the typing of the book: Mrs. Chris Ledger, my former secretary; Mrs. Doris Kay, of St. John's, Durham; Miss Chris Lunt, of the B.B.C. Manchester; and Mrs. Leslie Winsworth. My warm thanks go to those who have made helpful comments—Mr. Mike Roberts and Mr. Mark Townson—and to the wonderful and dear congregation of St. Nicholas', Durham, where Eileen and I served for seven hard but glorious years. A measure of the fellowship I have enjoyed from Catholic Christians may be gleaned from the fact that Ushaw Catholic Seminary in Durham made available to me their library and resources. I am deeply grateful to them and especially to Fr. Cuthbert Rand, one of the staff.

Chapter 1
THE
RENEWING
STREAM

*G*od has the knack of breaking into human history and upsetting our tidy systems. Church history provides ample evidence of this from the time of Jesus to the present day. We have only to think of the events of Pentecost, the oppression and persecution of the early church followed by the triumph of Christianity over paganism, the resurgence of Christianity in the Dark Ages, the rise of the reform movements in the Medieval Period, the Reformation and so on. At times God seems to wait until the situation seems totally hopeless. Then, to our astonishment and relief, he steps in.

God, it appears, is doing a work among denominations today which is in keeping with his activity in history. He is bringing us closer together. We are beginning to see our unity in Jesus, the common center of our faith. God is beginning to heal the self-inflicted wounds that have left us divided, scarred and weak. This is perhaps nowhere more apparent than in relations between Protestants and Roman Catholics. Dialog, sharing and cooperation take place at more levels today than would have been considered possible twenty-five years ago.

Indeed, that is where we must start—in dialog and sharing. Until

Vatican II the Roman Catholic Church was rigidly separated and isolated from Protestant churches. From one point of view this simplified things greatly because both sides were able to form clear, although distorted, impressions of one another. In Protestant eyes the Roman Catholic Church stood for a rigid, monolithic church government, which sprang from papal dictatorship. Lay people were cowed and dominated by a priestly cast which taught an unbiblical faith. Dogmas such as papal infallibility, the Immaculate Conception and bodily Assumption of the Virgin Mary were dismissed as totally alien to Scripture and the general tradition of the church. Furthermore, even if Protestants had no personal knowledge of what went on in Catholic worship, they were sure that it was superstitious nonsense.

From a Catholic perspective the picture of the Protestant churches was equally uncomplimentary. By leaving the true church Protestants had ended in heresy and confusion. Bible-thumping Protestants were to be avoided at all costs. Their naive and simplistic opinions made them no proper companions for thinking people. Their worship, furthermore, appeared to be democracy run riot with everyone doing his own thing. At the other end of the Protestant spectrum were Protestant liberals who were also dangerous, but for different reasons. They made reason their authority, thus appearing to dismiss the authority of church and Bible. Roman Catholics, therefore, saw nothing attractive in their Protestant counterparts. Protestantism was a world- and church-rejecting faith which made mournful and miserable Christians. In the words of Hilaire Belloc:

Where'er the Catholic sun does shine
There is music and laughter and good red wine,
At least I have always found it so—
Benedicamus Domino.

Such caricatures fulfilled a useful function for those anxious to maintain the "cold war" atmosphere. They were easily assimilated, and they inoculated Christians from really looking closely at what we agree about, as well as what separates us. Furthermore, they served to reinforce our acquired prejudices. They described clearly why we could never be a Protestant or a Catholic, since the pictures we held of one another were about as desirable as a holiday home in Siberia! Conceptually the caricatures successfully imprisoned those who might have been tempted to give a sympathetic hearing to a different point of view.

But times have changed. A new openness prevails and, as a result, these caricatures have been severely damaged if not destroyed. Two illustrations spring to mind. In November 1980 I and a team from my church in Durham led a conference on "Evangelism and Renewal" in Newcastle. Through teaching, drama and dance we endeavored to show what the Bible had to say about presenting the Christian faith and how we might use contemporary forms to do so. Over five hundred people attended the conference—at least sixty per cent of them Roman Catholic. Apart from the few nuns who stood out by reason of their dress, there was no way of telling which group was which. Although the Roman Catholics there were as staunchly committed to their church as ever, they brought their Bibles and spoke of a living faith in Christ. At another conference I led in Washington, near Newcastle, the organizer told me that a large number of Roman Catholics would be present and made this surprising comment: "You will recognize them at once because they are the keen evangelical ones!" And, sure enough, that is exactly what I found. Those who I might have thought were evangelical Christians because of their uninhibited manner of talking about their faith were in fact Roman Catholic Christians!

These are not isolated examples. In this book I want to argue that God's work of renewal is deeper and wider than many of us realize. At the same time, the challenges and problems—theological, liturgical and practical—that this renewal presents to ordinary Christians are more demanding than we might want.

What then, we must ask, are the central reasons for this growing together? What is the background to this stream of renewal?

The Reforming Council
The word *reformation* is not one we normally associate with the

Church of Rome, but it may be justly used of the Second Vatican Council which ran from 1962 to 1965. During that time the cardinals and bishops of the church met in the Vatican to deal with the theological and social issues facing the church. In its own right a Vatican council is a fairly unusual body. The cost and effort required keep the total hierarchy of the church from getting together frequently. Indeed, the last time such a council had been held was in 1870 when the infallibility of the Pope was proclaimed. What made Vatican II unusual was that it was essentially the vision of the elderly Pope John XXIII, who saw that his church faced a situation in the modern world unlike any other and that it required all the resources of the church to meet the challenge of the day.

Most people are familiar with the story of how Pope John, when asked by one of his cardinals to explain the purpose of the Second Vatican Council, replied by throwing open the window, saying simply, "We must let in fresh air." Not everyone agreed with him concerning the need to call a council, let alone that the church needed ventilation! On his appointment he was generally regarded to be a caretaker Pope, and caretakers do not normally initiate new things in any organization. When he announced to his closest advisers in the Curia his intention of holding a general council, they held their tongues, hoping that the old man would forget. But he had no intention of forgetting, and soon the idea became a reality.

With mounting excitement on the part of some and apprehension on the part of others, the Roman Catholic Church prepared for the great occasion. Excitement, however, turned into consternation within the first few days of the Council when the Curia presented the delegates with a prepared agenda and discussion papers. The delegates had no intention of being told what to do, and the prepared work was rejected and fresh agendas were prepared. The assembled Council revealed its mind that it was not going to be dictated to—the wind of change was blowing through the church, and the breath of the Spirit was shaking the structures.

Looking back on the Council now from the perspective of more than twenty years, we can see a little more clearly the changes that were taking place.[1]

The church began to listen to the world. Christians all too easily assume that God speaks only to them and through them and works only in the church. Somehow we think of the world as an evil, godless place which has rejected God. This is oversimplistic. While evil inhabits the world and the world is in need of salvation, it is still God's world and his Spirit works within it as well as within the church.

The Church of Rome, perhaps more than any other Christian denomination, kept itself aloof from the world. From the French Revolution on, it was left stranded by the rise of secular and scientific thought. It made little attempt to understand current movements in the world; on the contrary, it condemned the whole sweep of modernism.[2] This resulted in much of Catholicism being out of touch with the vast changes in society.

The question of authority inevitably faced the modern Roman Catholic Christian. Is the Pope alone the focus of authority? Isn't it rather naive and childish to look to just one man for one's authority in life? When the authority of the church is challenged by scientific authorities, what do we believe and what is our basis for believing?

The question of the relevance of the Christian faith was also at the forefront of the Council's thought. Many bishops were concerned by the church's failure to retain its grip on the minds and hearts of the young in Catholic countries, and desire to do something about this ran high. Many also wanted the church to tackle moral issues like contraception and abortion, but these were never officially considered and perhaps could not have been dealt with properly then.

But at the heart of all the issues and questions was the realization that the Church of Rome could no longer assume that it was the center of Christendom, which would in time conquer the world. The rise of atheism and secularism, the resurgence of other religions, the drift away from the church by many of the faithful made it clear that the old triumphalism no longer cut any ice. If the church was a Noah's ark, fewer and fewer wished to board her. Something had to be done. Even if the Council did not make many essential changes on moral issues, it adopted a healthier approach to the world: It realized that it had much to learn and that its structures had to change if this generation was to be influenced by the gospel. More important, the Council made it possible for Catholic Christians to ask questions that until then would have been frowned on.

Two main constitutions showed the concern that Catholic leaders felt about the importance of relating the faith to the world. The *Dogmatic Constitution on the Church* (known as *Lumen gentium*— "Light of Nations") reflects a major change in the church's understanding of itself. While the First Vatican Council of 1870 understood the church, as a hierarchical organization, static and institutionalized, this document emphasizes the church as the pilgrim people of God in history, sharing in Christ's ministry as prophet, priest and king. Its mission is to serve and bear witness to Christ. Furthermore, the whole church is involved in this task, lay people as well as clergy. Indeed, the document stresses the role of lay people in the church's mission.

The second constitution which bears on this theme, the *Pastoral Constitution on the Church in the Modern World* (known as *Gaudium et spes*—"Joy and Hope"), notes that the church exists not over the world, nor even alongside it, but within it as its servant, "to carry forward the work of Christ himself under the lead of the befriending Spirit."

Perhaps the most significant aspect about both constitutions is the spirit they exude. No longer does the triumphalism of Vatican I prevail, but instead we hear the voice of the church anxious to serve yet aware of the vast problems facing it in the world. In these documents we find a church no longer insular and shut away, but waking up to new opportunities and challenges.

The church began to listen to the Bible. The Church of Rome has always claimed that the Bible is its book and that the teaching of Scripture is at the heart of its theology and liturgy.

The problem, however, is that this claim looks very unconvincing in the light of the doctrines which the Catholic Church holds to be divinely revealed. "How can you say that your teaching is scriptural," non-Catholic Christians ask, "when so much of what you teach—the emphasis on the priesthood, the real presence, the Marian dogmas and the dogma of infallibility—seems so explicitly postbiblical?"

This question of authority poses one of the most important problems for unity and mutual understanding. Before the Second Vatican Council, Rome's teaching was based on a two-source theory of authority—Bible and tradition. The Council of Trent (1546-64) responded to the Reformation principle of *sola scriptura* by asserting the equality of Scripture and the unwritten apostolic tradition. The Tridentine confession of faith (1564) extended this to include ecclesiastical tradition: "The apostolic and ecclesiastical tradition and all other observances and constitutions of that same church I must firmly admit and embrace." In practice the equality of Scripture and tradition resulted in the subordination of the former to the latter, because who was to judge what was the correct teaching in any problem regarding interpretation? The answer was that the church itself decided on such matters through the teaching office (the magisterium), which was responsible for the sacred faith of the church. This body was the legitimate interpreter of Holy Scripture, and it decided whether or not church traditions were consonant with Holy Writ.[3]

It is difficult to avoid the conclusion that in this approach Scripture is a wax nose, capable of being moved by the predilection of the teaching office. There is a shade of this in the encyclical of Pope Leo XIII of 1893: "The Catholic scholar must follow the analogies of faith . . . and Catholic doctrine, as authoritatively proposed by the church . . . as the supreme law; for seeing that God is the author both of the sacred books and of the doctrine committed to the church, it is clearly impossible that any teaching can, by legitimate means, be extracted from the former, which shall in any respect, be at variance with the latter."

But by the time the Council began, it can be said fairly that many people in the church were unhappy about the rigidity of the church's teaching. In the period up to the Council many theologians and teachers had been reprimanded, disgraced or removed from office because of the challenges they brought to church teaching. But they could not be silenced completely because it was becoming more and more evident that if the church was going to be renewed, it had to go back to the source of its life in Scripture and get fresh directions. One of the great contributions of the Council was in fact its emphasis on Scripture and the importance of the Bible in theology, teaching and worship.

The *Dogmatic Constitution on Divine Revelation (Dei verbum*—"The Word of God") is one of the most important documents of the Council. Instead of repeating Trent's mistake of alluding to two sources of revelation, this constitution makes the point that there is one revelation of God, which is that of God in Christ. "By this revelation then, the deepest truth about God and the salvation of man is made clear to us in Christ, who is the Mediator and at the same time the fullness of all revelation."[4] He is the Word of God attested by Scripture and expressed in the church's traditions. Scripture in its witness to Christ is decisively important in guiding the belief and life of all Christians. Whether in testing established tradition, interpreting Christian experience or assessing other activities, the Bible is vital. It is a fixed point of reference. Being true to the Scripture means being true to one's original identity as a Christian.[5]

These sturdy, emphatic statements are heartening sentiments to the ears of other Christians. But it has to be said that the constitution is not completely satisfactory when it comes to the relationship between Bible and tradition. In fact, as we shall observe in greater detail later, the document is ambiguous, on the one hand wanting to hold on to the uniqueness of Scripture as normative for Christian truth, but on the other wanting to stress that Bible, tradition and the teaching office are equal authorities in the church and cannot be separated. We are back again with the same problem we noted earlier: Who is allowed the last word when it comes to deciding what is authentic doctrine?[6]

What is certain, however, is that the Council did place much greater importance on Scripture as the basis of theology and Christian truth. The consequence of this is most significant; the Council encouraged the laity to take Scripture more seriously, to read it daily and to give it a central place in private prayer. Similarly the clergy were urged to "share the abundant wealth of the divine word."[7]

Such willing exposure to the Bible means new possibilities and fresh challenges. In taking the Bible seriously, Roman Catholics realize at once that they have something in common with their separated brethren in other churches. The Bible is God's secret uniting weapon. It is the common source book of the Christian church. But more uncomfortably Roman Catholics, by taking the Bible deep into their private lives, become aware that the Bible challenges their assumptions, practices and theology just as it challenges those of Protestants. Both must face tough questions: Is your faith biblical? Do your cherished beliefs find their roots in New Testament Christianity?

The church began to listen to other churches. When Vatican II began, it was almost as if all other churches did not really exist. The traditional Catholic approach was that there was only one church in God's eyes—the Holy Roman Church, which was united in the papal office based on the apostle Peter. Rome's attitude to the problem of disunity was devastatingly simple and uncompromisingly clear "Return to the Holy Catholic Church." With this simple and clear but unbending stand, Rome saw no reason for dialog because it possessed the truth and its ministry alone sacramentally conveyed God's grace. Protestants have always been amazed at this seemingly arrogant position, but the Catholic Church has never intended to be taken in that way—such an attitude simply expressed its conviction that other Christian bodies and sects had deviated from the fullness of Catholicism and that unity was a simple matter of the prodigal returning home.

Vatican II treated the problem differently. First, it addressed the problem of history to which we shall turn in the next chapter. Pope Paul VI in his opening speech on September 29, 1963, publicly acknowledged that the Church of Rome must accept its share of responsibility for past dissensions among Christians. Turning to the non-Catholic observers he said, "If we are in any way to blame for the fact that we are separated, I humbly beg God's forgiveness and ask pardon of our separated brethren who feel that they have been injured by us." Later speakers congratulated Pope Paul for this amazing public statement of contrition.

The Decree on Ecumenism, according to Walter Abbott, S. J., marks
the full entry of the Roman Catholic Church into the ecumenical
movement.[8] In this document the Council goes beyond the assertion
that the Catholic Church is the one and only true church to stress that
God is at work in the churches beyond its visible borders. It
acknowledges that disunity prevents the Roman Catholic Church
from expressing its full catholicity. Oscar Cullmann says of the
contribution of the decree that "this is more than the opening of a
door: new ground has been broken. No Catholic document has ever
spoke of non-Catholic Christians in this way."[9]

The change from pre-Vatican II days is also evident in the Council's
different approach to the church. While the church had before been
considered a monolithic and unchanging body, the Council now saw
the church as consisting of sinful, fallible people who in their
pilgrimage were handing on God's truth in Christ. This note of the
pilgrim church dominated the Council and has had major repercussions on modern thinking concerning the nature of the Christian
community. If the church is composed of sinful people on their way
to the true kingdom, does it not suggest that the truth is shared? That
perhaps the separated brethren are not completely in the dark?

Then there was the realization that when we talk of Christian truth
we are really talking not of Christian teaching, packaged and
processed like goods in a supermarket, but of truth about a person,
namely, Jesus Christ. It is not enough to talk about faith; faith has to
be lived and love has to be shared. "Let all Christ's faithful remember
that the more purely they strive to live according to the gospel, the
more they are fostering and even practicing Christian unity."[10] Such
gospel living requires a change of heart, sympathetic study of the
beliefs of separated brethren, and worship together whenever possible.
This the decree calls "spiritual ecumenism."[11]

Some Protestant theologians, especially more conservative ones,
have argued that Vatican II changed little. There is the same basic
doctrine, they argue. The leopard has not changed its spots; it is only
subdued. While there remains justification for their concerns and
many issues still divide us, we need to see that Vatican II created a

milieu that has made it possible for the Roman Catholic Church to change and other churches to influence it and be influenced themselves. Just as social changes in the late eighteenth century made it possible for the Industrial Revolution to be really effective in England, so Vatican II has introduced an environment which has given theology greater freedom, leading to major changes in worship as well as outlook.

Conservative Protestants are not the only ones who have viewed the post-Vatican II era with suspicion. For many Catholics, the Council and the years of change that have followed have been painful as well as exciting, disturbing as well as hopeful. William McSweeney laments, "The effect of the Second Vatican Council is negative rather than positive and it is thoroughly modern: the authority to dissent."[12] The repercussions of the Second Vatican Council are still being experienced today, and they are momentous for the whole Christian body.

The Reviving Spirit
In 1952 Bishop Lesslie Newbigin made theologians sit up with his statement that there are three great Christian movements in the modern world: a Catholic "Sacramental" movement, a Protestant "Word" movement and a Pentecostal "Spirit" movement.[13] At the time Pentecostalism had quite a hold on emergent Christian communities in Latin America, but as a movement could it lay claim to the greatness of the other two? Few would challenge that claim today. Pentecostalism has moved a long way from its rather unlikely beginnings in Kansas and California to the modern charismatic movement, which has made inroads into practically every church and tradition.

Why is this? Some of the reasons we have already touched on; the ground was already being prepared by the inability of both Protestant and Catholic communities to really share the faith with the outside world. Confidence was shattered, and more and more people felt that the church's resources were at an end. Brokenness served as a prelude to God's power.

But there was a second factor. If God was saying to his people "not by might, not by power, but my Spirit," he was also saying that the Christian ministry is not limited to ordained clerics but is for all. It is startling to discover that the Reformation changed little as far as the role of the laity was concerned. If it was possible for a Pope in the thirteenth century to say that the role of the laity was "to turn up, pay up, and shut up," so to speak, the Reformation did not significantly alter the passive nature of the "learning" church. The preacher replaced the priest, and the layman sat under the Word as he had sat under the Mass. The priesthood of all believers means that everyone has access to God through Christ and human mediation is unnecessary for salvation. But somehow Christians at the time of the Reformation failed to see that it also means that everyone has a role in Christian ministry and that the gifts of the Spirit are available for exercise in the church.[14] The charismatic movement has broadened our view of the priesthood of all believers, and in both Protestant and Roman Catholic communities it has led to a rediscovery of lay people and their role in church and world.

The heart of the charismatic movement, or the renewal movement as it is sometimes called, lies in the conviction that the formal, stylish and secondhand religion of much contemporary Christianity is a far cry from the vigorous, throbbing faith of the New Testament. God can be known in his power, and the gifts and graces of the Holy Spirit are available today as they were long ago. Not surprisingly, charismatics have concentrated on the more ecstatic side of New Testament faith—speaking in tongues, miracles and so on. The distinguishing feature of the movement, it is claimed, is the baptism of the Spirit, which is usually marked by the gift of tongues. While this may be the hallmark at the sharp end of the movement, at the broadest and most popular end is a deep desire for the church to return to New Testament experience, the simplicity of faith and a new openness to the Holy Spirit.

Charismatic renewal, of course, raises many theological issues and challenges that we cannot discuss here, but the movement clearly has had and is having considerable impact on dialog among Christians.

It is the only revival in history which has united evangelicals on the one hand, with their strong emphasis on the death of Christ and full atonement, and Roman Catholics on the other, with their emphasis on the sacraments. Somehow charismatic experiences have brought together people who on the face of it have little in common theologically.

As I write I think of a prominent man in my congregation who for years was a rigid Reformed man, hidebound in a tradition which rejected Catholicism outright. His Christianity was so narrow and insular that it allowed him contact only with like-minded people. But his life changed in a remarkable way. He went to the United States on a lecture tour, and he met a group of charismatic Christians who led him into an experience of the Holy Spirit that revolutionized his theology. No longer narrow, this man is an open Christian, expressing great joy and love in a liberated life. His love of the Bible is just as great as before, and his hold on biblical doctrines such as justification by faith is just as strong. But his charismatic experience is a bridge which has brought him closer to other Christians. That kind of transformation is common today, and in prayer gatherings in many parts of the world Protestants and Catholics meet together to share the faith and show their unity to the world. Indeed, these prayer gatherings show how tiny the steps are that churches are making toward one another in *Agreed Statements* and so on. Theological dialog is, of course, important and must continue, but at the grassroots level the Spirit is moving and already taking many Christians to a level of spiritual unity far deeper than the union of ecclesiastical bodies.

Recurrent Problems
It is all too easy for Christians to slip into simplistic solutions about unity. "All one in Christ Jesus" can be a motto for a naive Christianity which ignores real issues and bypasses great opportunities. Charismatics have been guilty of having an experience-centered faith which is the be-all and end-all of their Christian lives. When their church no longer meets their needs, they look for a different church or group which will give them the experiences they desire. Denominational

doctrine no longer matters—it's the Spirit that counts. Evangelicals, similarly, have been guilty of the same tendency, although for different reasons. They have rushed to find a "pure" church which teaches the "truth." Sometimes they have been disappointed to find that new churches are not greatly different from the ones they have left.

Likewise young Christians, converted at university or college and nurtured in substitute churches like Christian unions, chaplaincies and other campus fellowships, often leave college thinking that where they worship does not really matter. The situation we find ourselves in today makes it easier for, say, a Protestant to consider becoming a Roman Catholic and vice versa. The openness to one another has opened up greater access between denominations. There is much good in this trend, but there are dangers as well.

One danger is that we ignore the real theological issues which still separate us and which are still important because they represent unresolved conflict. Theological truth is important, and nothing is to be gained by pretending that we are more enlightened than our forbears and share a wonderful unity. Another danger is to ignore the historical and cultural traditions that shape us and which can so easily limit our appreciation of other ways of viewing reality, thus leading to prejudice and bigotry. As I type this book I am conscious that I am shaped by my personal Christian history. I came from a non-churchgoing family in the East End of London (a true Cockney!), and I was led to faith through an Anglican evangelical church. Since then I have been influenced by both the charismatic and ecumenical movements. Such things have not only influenced me but made it possible for these things to limit me. I could easily look at other Christians and judge them because they do not think the way I think or act as I act.

Such problems throw up interesting questions concerning our relationships with other Christians. Let me give two examples.

Phil was raised in the Roman Catholic Church. While at university he made an adult commitment to Christ through the caring attention of his college Christian union. Later he was able to explain that the formalized faith of his Catholic background had become alive. Jesus was no longer a figure in history but a reality in daily life. The Holy Spirit was now the Spirit of power, no longer merely an element in the creed. As he worshiped with my congregation he gradually realized he could no longer continue as a Roman Catholic. He had shifted so greatly—theologically and temperamentally—that I felt it was right to receive him into the Church of England.

Anne, however, presented me with a different set of questions. Unlike Phil, her Roman Catholicism was strong and deep. On coming to Durham University she received a warm welcome from her Christian union and started attending my church. In time she developed a lively faith and came to see me about becoming an Anglican. As we discussed this together I became hesitant about doing as she wished. I could not deny her faith in Christ, but her understanding of the church was so slight. What would happen to her when she left university and the fellowship of my church? If she became an Anglican, how would it affect her relationship with her family? And would becoming an Anglican keep her from working out her discipleship as a renewed Roman Catholic Christian? I put it to her that it would be best if she stayed a Catholic for the time being but that she would still be welcome at my church and could participate fully in our life. She was initially very disappointed. Later developments, however, seem to confirm my counsel. The following academic year she spent in France, and the only lively Christian fellowship in the place where she lived was a Roman Catholic church. She returned to Durham more appreciative of the tradition which had reared her, while at the same time just as secure in her faith.

Many might fault me for not encouraging her to leave a church which in their opinion is unreformed. I can only reply that more trouble is caused by "church-hopping" than by most other practices or issues. There is really little to commend the ecclesiastical game of "cowboys and Indians" in which churches raid each other's traditions to take "hostages." While there will always be people like Phil who think through the issues deeply and come to a decision to change their spiritual home, there will be people like Anne who will not fit our convenient ecclesiastical planning.

Church leaders and all thinking Christians need to reflect on the new situation we are in and consider what policies we should employ to embody the Christian hope that we share. Can we any longer live and act as if only we have Christian truth and that other Christians, somehow, are imposters? The history of our separation is so important to this issue. No church begins de novo. Because we are in history, we carry forward the seeds of destruction as well as hope. "Those who reject history," said Santayana, "are condemned to repeat it." To this legacy of history we turn in the next chapter.

Chapter 2
TROUBLED
WATERS

Seemingly ordinary objects can arouse different and sometimes competing emotions. Take a motorbike. To Andy, a young friend of mine, his motorbike represents power, status and great pleasure. He is in a world of his own when he is speeding along the highway at 90 mph. This gleaming, powerful machine symbolizes the macho life he dreams about. But to his mother that same object is a smelly, noisy and frightening beast. It represents dirty, oily clothes and, most important, the fear that Andy might injure himself one day. We can all think of other ordinary objects that can be the focus of both admiration and disgust. It all depends, we say, on our perspective.

The Reformation is rather like that. For Protestants it is an important part of their history. It represents the break from the power of the Roman Church, the rediscovery of the Bible and the recovery of the central truths of the Christian faith. For Roman Catholics, however, the Reformation represents something quite different. It is a tragedy, a tear in the body of Christ, a regrettable step that has isolated the Protestant churches from the true life of the Catholic Church. For one side, the Reformation spells freedom, life and vitality; for the other, separation, schism and sadness.

And we all must acknowledge that the Reformation *was* a sad episode in the history of Christianity. Even today its distant echo is heard in our divisions. No part of the globe has resisted its influence. This aspect of European history, at least, still pervades the Christianity of the Americas, Africa, Asia and Australia. We may be tempted to look back and dismiss the squabbles between those sixteenth-century Christians as tiresome and petty arguments of little consequence today. But we cannot dismiss the Reformation so easily. It went to the heart of the Christian gospel and it raised crucial issues: What is salvation? What is the content of the Christian good news? How can we find God and know him? Where does ultimate authority lie for the Christian?

In this chapter we are going to ferret out a bit of history to see what the Reformation issues were and how far we have got in resolving them. Certain aspects may seem strange if we have never delved deeply into these matters before. But if we are able to persevere, we will better understand the issues involved.

The hero or villain of the piece—again depending on your perspective—is Martin Luther. Martin Luther was an Augustinian monk, a brilliant scholar who eventually became professor of Holy Scripture at the University of Wittenberg. If anyone had a great future in the church, he had. But Luther was troubled by the great weight placed on ordinary people to respond to Rome's financial demands. He was not alone in this. The early part of the sixteenth century was a time of questioning and searching. The human spirit was on the move. All the old authorities were being examined critically, even the church. As it happened, the issue of indulgences became the snapping point.

For years the bureaucracy of Rome had been living beyond its means. Corruption was rife in the church; minor officials commonly took their cut of papal fees and taxes. The Pope consequently incurred most of the blame but little of the financial reward. Spiraling costs forced the Popes to take desperate measures. Pope Alexander VI pawned his tiara in 1494 for 100,000 ducats. Alexander was succeeded by Julius II, who continued the policy of lavish spending by his patronage of the Renaissance arts. He was especially generous to Raphael, Michelangelo and Bramante. But patronage costs money.

By the time Pope Leo X came to office in 1513 the kitty was nearly exhausted, and the vast, new, unfinished basilica of St. Peter's in Rome had still to be paid for. How many tourists and pilgrims praying in and looking over the splendid basilica of St. Peter's realize that that building was the innocent, though precipitate, cause of the Reformation? It probably would have happened anyway, but this was the straw that broke the camel's back. A ready-made solution to the problem of St. Peter's was at hand in the shape of indulgences. By the simple offering of money, the faithful could be reassured that the souls of their loved ones could be released from purgatory and repose in peace. "When the coin in the coffer rings, a soul from purgatory springs." Apart from the evil of a system which bred a mixture of fear and love, the practice fostered the belief that forgiveness could be bought.

This mounting campaign of indulgences, which swept through Europe to fill the coffers of Rome, coincided with a critical event in the life of Martin Luther: He discovered the real secret of Christianity—faith in Jesus Christ. Luther was obsessed with the search for God. He tried everything that his Augustinian discipline demanded, but his soul could find no peace until the day he read in Romans "the just shall live by faith." Out of this sprang a new understanding of faith. Does it rest in me, the church, or what? He saw that there could be only one center to faith—Jesus Christ. Jesus alone can save, and by faith in him alone can we live.

The break came in October 1517 when to the door of Wittenberg Castle Luther pinned his ninety-five theses, attacking the sale of indulgences. But, as people realized at the time, Luther's attack on indulgences sprang out of conviction that God's forgiveness was not an external thing which the church could give away, but an internal transaction between God and the sinner. Much to his surprise, Luther found himself in conflict with the full might and authority of his church, and the Reformation began.[1]

Before continuing our study of the issues which divide Catholics and Protestants, we must remind ourselves that we are not contrasting a Catholic horror show with a Protestant paradise. Nearly everyone today agrees that at the Reformation the church was at one of its most degenerate points, largely due to a combination of political, social and theological factors. Few at the time, with the possible exception of Erasmus, anticipated the approaching explosion. We must be careful not to allow our view of Catholicism to be colored by its sixteenth-century appearance. Likewise modern Protestantism must not be confused with the pristine Christian communities of the Reformation. Ultimately, while we must learn from all periods of the past, we must remember that we are children of this age and apply the timeless principles of the gospel to our generation.

The Reformation exposed some of those timeless gospel principles clearly. Four of the most important I have shown diagramatically in figure 1.

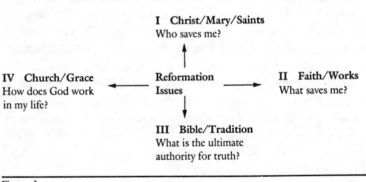

Figure 1.

In this chapter we shall glance briefly at these four questions raised by the Reformation challenge and then consider the first three in greater depth in the following chapter.

Who Saves Me?

In the late Medieval Period Jesus Christ, although regarded as Savior and Redeemer, seemed very austere and distant to the average Christian. Contact with him or with the benefits of his salvation was thought possible only through Mary or one of the saints. Perhaps an overemphasis on Jesus' divinity contributed to this. "He is the divine Son of God, so how can he understand me and my problem? But Mary, she's different—warm, maternal, comforting—she can intercede for me because she knows all about human suffering." Popular piety jumped readily to that kind of conclusion, even if it wasn't put in exactly those words.

Luther's own experience of God led him to a Christ-centered faith. Christ is the absolute heart of Christianity; he is its essence and fullness. "In Christ I have the Father's heart and will," Luther said. Christ is the sole revealer of God and the only mediator between God and us. As Luther saw it, this is the touchstone of New Testament faith. From this the Reformers deduced that the Bible gives no basis for the worship of either Mary or the saints. Indeed, they ventured to argue, to elevate Mary or other great pioneers of faith can only threaten the pre-eminence of Christ and blur his unique role.

Squabbles so often heighten points of difference instead of revealing common ground, with separated parties taking up defensive positions around precious viewpoints from which they will not budge. Fossilization thus sets in. In just this way the rift between Catholics and Protestants over the place of Mary widened during the sixteenth century. In reaction to the Catholic emphasis Protestants practically ignored the Virgin Mary and her place in the church while Catholic piety accelerated in the opposite direction, even to the point of calling her co-mediator with Christ.

The place of Mary in the church, then, is a major source of disagreement between the two great Christian traditions. If Mary is seen to hold a mediating role in the work of salvation—that is, a role through whom someone comes to God or through whom salvation is given—we must recognize that this is a deviation from Scripture and foreign to the thought and practice of the Christian church for practically the first thousand years. The problem is compounded further by two dogmas which have increased the status of Mary within the Roman Church—the dogma of the Immaculate Conception of Mary and the dogma of her bodily Assumption into heaven. Many modern Roman Catholics are uncomfortably aware of the difficulties these beliefs cause Protestants. How can Protestants subscribe to the idea that Mary was conceived without sin when no scriptural support exists? And then again, how can Protestants be asked to believe that she did not die but was translated into heaven bodily when a deafening silence comes from the Bible?

What Saves Me?

As we observed earlier, Luther found the key to Christianity in faith in Christ alone. If he is the only Savior, then it follows that only through him can a person know God. Faith—that is, personal trust—in Christ is all God requires.

The Medieval understanding of salvation was based on two doctrines: the doctrine of works and that of the church. Eternal life was gained by a worthy life nourished through the ministries of the church. Rules and regulations had replaced freedom and grace in the Christian life. A clerically controlled penitential system gave the impression that salvation could only be earned by a life of good works linked with grace flowing through the sacramental life of the church. Good deeds, therefore, became the *root* and not, as the New Testament regards it, the *fruit* of salvation. A moralistic gospel prevailed in which people believed that they were saved by living virtuous lives. Christ may have won universal salvation, but the individual was saved only through faithful conformity to his example and obedience to the teaching of the church.

Luther discovered the errors of such Medieval Christianity only gradually. He was an earnest friar, practicing the prayers of the church and zealous in good works. But his conscience reminded him of his failure to live up to God's standard of holiness. It kept telling him: "You fell short there. You left that sin off your list, didn't you? You can't conquer temptation. You are a failure." He felt God-forsaken. His life was transformed, though, when he discovered that the word *faith* in the New Testament means trust in Christ's victory on the cross. Of course! Christ's righteousness is made available to all who ask. Faith is the channel through which the grace of Jesus finds me.

Forgiveness cannot be won; it is a gift!

The Reformation, in fact, focused on one word—*justification*. For the Reformers, faith alone justifies a person, and they pointed to the many texts in Galatians and Romans which appear to confirm this idea: "A man is justified by faith apart from works of law" (Rom 3:28). "Therefore, since we are justified by faith, we have peace with God through our Lord Jesus Christ" (Rom 5:1). For them it meant being made right, acquitted through the work of Jesus Christ and set free. Just as an offender might go scot-free through the intervention of a friend who pays his fine, Christ has paid in full the penalty of our sins and misdeeds so that we might be forgiven and liberated from the tyranny of the past. Justification is wholly of God—that is, by grace—and it is obtained through faith.[2]

This concept of justification was at loggerheads with Catholic doctrine. Although Catholic teaching was just as emphatic on the primacy of God's grace in salvation, it held that justifying grace flowed sacramentally through the church. Justification was therefore seen as an ongoing transformation of the individual which starts with the sacrament of baptism and culminates on earth with the last rites.

This notion of justification as a process was refuted by Luther, who asserted that it is not a process but a declaration of our acquittal through Christ. While Catholic teaching located justification in the experience of the believer, Luther located it in the merits of Christ which are made ours through his death. We are therefore declared righteous on the basis of what God had done in Christ. We have no righteousness of our own, but Christ's righteousness is *imputed* to us. We are always, declared Luther, *"simul justus et peccator"*—at one and the same time righteous and sinful. In ourselves we are unworthy of salvation, but in Christ we are heirs of salvation.

Although this issue may seem simple and straightforward to us now, it was certainly not in the Reformation period. The Reformers seemed to be preaching a subversive message which undermined the authority of the church and questioned its role of ministering God's grace to people. Church leaders were disturbed by the individualism of the teaching which made the faith of the believer all-important and which denied the role of the church in salvation. Searching questions were put to this new movement: If my faith is all-important, doesn't this make Christianity highly subjective? Can we really be sure of salvation? Isn't it arrogant to say, "I am saved"? Doesn't faith in Christ alone bypass the church and its ordained ministry of priests and sacraments? These questions were not dealt with in a calm way by Christians looking at the evidence and trying to reach a solution which would satisfy both sides. The political and religious uproar of the times prevented such objectivity. Emotion ruled and within a few years Luther was excommunicated and his teaching anathematized.[3]

Looking back we can sympathize with both sides. Catholics had reason to wonder how the doctrine of faith alone was compatible with the idea of the church as a body and to wonder how people could without presumption be certain of heaven. From the Reformers' point of view justification by faith appeared to be the straightforward message of Scripture that had been obscured by the church's teaching that good deeds and fidelity to the church were required.

What Is the Ultimate Authority for Truth?

Although we live in an age which distrusts authority, even the most radical freedom fighter cannot altogether dispense with it. We find ourselves accepting authority when we need information concerning trains to catch, when we learn a new skill, even when we try out a scientific hypothesis. Life is too short to test everything. We accept authority when it coincides with our understanding of reality.

Christians need authorities as well. The gospel does not come to us as a made-up package like detergent—it comes in the Bible and through the church. Although reason plays an important part in our acceptance of it, we know that without the Holy Spirit we are blind and helpless. But the moment we become Christians we place ourselves under God's authority in the church.

Protestants and Catholics have differed in their views about God's authority and how it comes to us. Let us look at the traditional caricatures—mind you, they are only caricatures, and few of us would wish to identify simply with what follows. They do, however, serve a useful purpose in highlighting traditional assumptions, as well as showing, as we look back, how far we have come in recent years.

Protestants are caricatured as Bible-thumpers. Scripture is their authority and their test is simply this: Has this teaching got sufficient support in Scripture for it to become doctrine? Protestants, especially if they belong to mainstream denominations, do not ignore the teaching of the church in its creeds and its ancient statements, but they regard them only as supplements which confirm the teaching of the Bible.

Catholics, on the other hand, are caricatured as a group who replaces Scripture by tradition. Rather than just confirming and strengthening Scripture, tradition is believed to have a crucial role in developing Christian doctrine and even adding to biblical truth.

The caricatures suggest that Protestants have only one authority and that Catholics have two. Protestants rely on Scripture which stands over tradition and assesses it. Catholics, however, are believed to rely on a two-source approach to revelation which comes from Scripture and tradition.

Although this is a bald outline of the traditional differences on authority, it summarizes the basic problem which existed before the Second Vatican Council. We can see how difficult it was for Catholics and Protestants to find common ground when there was no agreement concerning how to test what is true or false. For example, how could agreement be found on the Marian dogmas when Catholics appealed not to Scripture but to church traditions, which Protestants rejected as an unreliable guide?

But let us go back to the Reformation. It is sometimes said that the Reformers replaced an infallible Pope with an infallible Bible. In fact, this is not the case: All scholars at the time accepted the authority of Scripture, and, in principle, the Reformers did not differ from Catholics concerning its status. The Bible was the Word of God for all. The difference between the two sides lay in how they thought the Bible should function in the church.

The Reformers considered the Bible to be the final and complete Word of God; it was less a textbook of doctrine and more a personal communication from God. It was less a revelation of intellectual formulas and more the story of the glorious experience of salvation which all could share.

Medieval theology had erected an intimidating theological tower which only intellectuals and the initiated could enter. It had built a concept of Christianity that consisted of rules and regulations. Mystery surrounded the Christian faith; the ordinary person sought light by accepting the authority of the church.

From one point of view the discovery of the Bible as God's Word which spoke now to human hearts was a form of *reductionism*. It questioned other authority structures, swept away unbiblical practices and put into the hands of ordinary people a tool to test religious dogmas. Johann Eck, Martin Luther's great opponent, saw with alarm what was happening and commented: "Things have come to a sorry state when even women answer back doctors of the law by quoting the Bible back at them!"

How Does God Work in My Life?
Perhaps like me you have been to a function that you have found utterly strange. You have wanted to get out as quickly as possible, leaving what seems so alien to get back to the security of more familiar culture. This strong sense of something alien often overcomes Roman Catholics or Protestants in attending worship in one another's culture. As most Protestants stand in a Catholic church and observe the important elements of Catholic worship— holy water, statues, candles, pictures and images of the saints, the altar and tabernacle, vestments and so on—they sense the otherness of the Roman Catholic faith. Most Catholics find Protestant worship equally strange. They find few religious symbols and wonder if Protestants have so internalized and individualized the Christian faith that they are left with no external props.

Neither Protestant nor Catholic observers would doubt the sincerity and devotion of the other, but both might properly ask: What is at the heart of this division in religious practice?

We shall look at three areas which have separated us and try to explore the nature of the differences.

Grace and Sacraments. The church of the sixteenth century considered its main role to lie in communicating God's grace to its flock. This was the assumption behind indulgences. Leaving aside the rights or wrongs of offering forgiveness or remission from judgment to those already dead, the implicit understanding at the time was that the church had power with God to give life to others. The main way that God's grace came was through the sacraments of the church. The Reformers did not challenge the assumption that God uses church rites and ministry—this they held in common with Catholics—but they did question the notion that the grace of God was conveyed automatically.

At the time of the Reformation (and for a long time after) the Catholic understanding was that grace is given *ex opere operato* (literally, "by the work worked"—that is, through the appointed means of grace). The common view in the church was that the sacrament was sufficient; it was a channel between God and humankind, and as such it affected what it reached. Not everyone in the church at the time agreed. Many who did not follow Luther into open revolt with the church agreed with him that a sacrament needs the personal response of faith. God's grace, Luther argued, does not dispense with my assent but requires it. Grace and faith must meet—this is the gospel, he asserted.

These two terms became the cornerstone of Reformation theology and are still at the heart of Protestant theology. "*By* grace, *through* faith" was the Protestant rallying cry in the sixteenth and seventeenth centuries. Although (as with so many catch phrases) it quickly became abused as the basis for witch hunts to distinguish the "saved" from the "unsaved," it expressed an important New Testament truth: that God's salvation is a free gift and depends from beginning to end on God's *grace* in Christ. This gift, though, must

be humbly accepted. Our acceptance is our response of *faith*. Today
we see that to hold this understanding is not necessarily to take sides,
because Catholic and Protestant insights taken together suggest a
more balanced interpretation of grace and faith. Grace is not
automatic. Here the Reformers were right in pointing out the
potential abuse of such a stand. But, equally, faith is not individualistic, as Catholic theologians were as quick to remark. Grace and
faith come to us within the Christian community. This is the context
in which God's grace is experienced and our faith begins and grows.

The Mass. Reformation teaching on grace and faith had profound
consequences for worship. For a start, it challenged the Roman
Catholic teaching about the Mass. At the time of the Reformation
the Eucharist was understood as the sacrament where Christ was
"re-presented" to the Father by the priest. This bloodless sacrifice
made Christ available to God's people once the substance of the
bread was changed into the substance of Christ. The Reformers and
their followers took issue with this physicalist doctrine known as
"transubstantiation." Their questions were severe and disturbing.
How can Christ be reoffered when the New Testament tells us that
his sacrifice is complete and final? How can the substance of Christ
be *in* a bread wafer? And concerning the role of the priest, what
justification have we to reduce the Christian ministry to the
unbiblical notion that its main role is the priestly offering of the
Mass?

Protestants were united in their agreement that the Holy Communion service was not a sacrifice or a reoffering except in special
senses, but rather a service of remembrance, thanksgiving and praise.
But this basic agreement among the Reformers on what it was
not did not lead to full agreement on what Holy Communion was.
Zwingli, the Swiss Reformer, believed that the Holy Communion was a powerful memorial, but yet a memorial only, of Christ's
death. Luther, on the other hand, could not agree and came closer
to some aspects of the Catholic position by teaching that Christ was
sacramentally present *with* the elements. And there were many other
interpretations in between.

Attitudes of Worship. To a large extent the differences which divide Christians to this day are expressed in the things we say about God when we worship. Worship, we might say, is the printout of our theological data. Beliefs are programmed in and worship emerges as data.

Protestant worship following the Reformation focused on Bible teaching and sharing. Because Christianity was seen as something done by God and given by God, worship centered on the Word of God. Positive aspects of this included deep fellowship, close knowledge of the Bible and high standards of private morality. Weaknesses included a tendency toward a subjective, privatized religion which shunned contact with the "sinful" world of secular life. In its anxiety to contradict the "Catholic" notion of a real presence of Christ in the sacrament of Holy Communion, it seemed to teach a real absence.

The printout of Catholicism also had its positive and negative sides. Positively Catholics emphasized God's activity in worship. People came expecting to meet God sacramentally, and they did not go away disappointed. The element of mystery was important in the Catholic notion of worship and was reinforced by the Latin rite, the numerous rituals and the ornately garbed priest. This element has given to Catholics a deep and indelible sense of the supernatural. As a friend of mine remarked as we entered a Roman Catholic church and saw a nun praying before a crucifix, "Catholics have been taught to adore." This attitude has been more caught than taught. Solidity and unity focused on the priest and the Mass have also characterized Catholic worship, which has comforted and reassured the faithful. Negatively the printout has its disturbing features in a dominant priesthood within an authoritarian concept of ministry, resulting in a largely untaught laity, and a formidable and rigid belief structure.

Even today the principal differences between Catholics and Protestants are expressed in worship. It would be wrong to suggest that somehow we are just the same. But there has been a true growing together nevertheless. If we take the sacrament of Holy Communion—the Lord's Supper, the Mass, the Breaking of Bread, the Eucharist, or whatever terminology we use—Protestants and Catholics will agree that this sacrament is a unique and indispensable rite where Christians meet their Lord, feed on him by faith and are strengthened to serve him. Protestants appreciate more today the Catholic emphasis on this service, and in many Protestant circles Catholic insights have been embraced, such as more reverence in sacramental worship, greater frequency in taking communion and so on. On the other hand, Catholics recognize that the risen Christ cannot be localized in the wafer. He is the Host at the sacramental meal as well as the Gift appropriated by faith. The charismatic movement has had a significant part in this story too, because as charismatic Christians have come together in one another's churches they have begun to spot the similarities and appreciate each other's emphases.

We have glanced at four Reformation issues which are still important for Christian unity today, and in the following chapters we will consider some of them more closely. But for the moment we observe with sadness a divided Christian world which, instead of serving the world from the strength of its unity, carries on in the weakness of its separation and sin. Today we experience the poignancy of the saying that the past makes us what we are. It is irreversible, and we suffer the consequences of past actions. Four hundred years of bitterness, misunderstanding and separate cultural growth cannot be removed overnight. But love has a way of overcoming barriers long before theological orthodoxy has found the right-length ladder. It is to the quest of mutual understanding that we now turn.

Chapter 3
CURRENTS OF
FAITH

*I*t is now time to explore more closely some of the issues raised in the last chapter. As we do so we are tackling subjects intimately associated with our spiritual lives. We may consider the other point of view misguided, heretical and wrong—nevertheless, whatever our estimate, we must be sensitive to the fact that we are handling deep-seated, precious ideas which cannot be simply brushed aside. Such currents of faith may be in collision with our own, but unity can only flow from a sympathetic and honest appraisal of the problems linked, as it ought to be, with a desire to find God's truth.

The Marian Dimension and Its Challenge to Christ

We ended the introduction to the last chapter with a question which expresses the heart-searching of Protestants who long for unity. How can we accept Roman Catholic dogmas about Mary when the New Testament has so little to say about her? If the dogmas of her Immaculate Conception and bodily Assumption, and her role in mediation, are nonnegotiable and must be held by all Christians, then Protestants must press home the point that at the very least we should have expected God to give us a clear biblical witness.

We look, however, in vain for such evidence. Instead the New Testament is consistently Christocentric in its outlook. The salvation of the world is through him alone (Acts 4:12); he is the sole mediator (1 Tim 2:5); no other foundation can be laid for our salvation (1 Cor 3:11). Mary, on the other hand, is not at all central in the Gospels. It would appear from Mark, the earliest Gospel, that she was ignorant of her son's mission before the resurrection. Rather than encouraging devotion to his mother and family, Jesus deflects adulation away from them. To the statement "your mother and brothers are outside, asking for you," Jesus replies, "Who is my mother and my brothers? . . . Whoever does the will of God is my brother, and sister, and mother."

A clear and firm perspective on Mary emerges, in fact, from the New Testament. In no way was she a leading figure in the early church, and at no point is there evidence that veneration of Mary was encouraged. She was certainly "highly favored" and chosen for a unique role in God's plan of salvation (Lk 1:28). She is an inspiring example of humility in submitting to God's will, which was to bring the Savior of the world into the world. But in the infancy narrative the spotlight falls on the Son and not the mother. The Scriptures support the view that following the birth of Jesus Mary's work was over, and she retreats into the shadows so that all may see her son more clearly.

In the early church Mariology developed from Christology. In A.D. 451 Nestorius's teaching that Mary was the "mother of Christ" was rejected in favor of Cyril's infelicitous phrase that Mary was the "mother of God." Cyril's attention was not in fact on Mary in the first place but on Jesus. Against Nestorius's teaching, which led back to a human Jesus, Cyril fought tenaciously for the full deity of Christ, and he saw it essential to maintain that Mary did not bear a human messiah but the Son of God himself. She was not merely the "bearer of Christ" (*christotokos*), she was the "bearer of God" (*theotokos*) because the person she gave birth to was none other than the divine Son of God who is worthy of all honor and worship.

While theologically this phrase protected the full divinity of Jesus, it had an important side effect in fanning the devotion to Mary which had become an important strand in popular piety at the time. While the veneration of Mary increased in the Middle Ages, no new dogmas about her were promulgated then. Not until the nineteenth century did the Catholic church formally take the development of Marian theology a step further—and, sadly, one step further away from unity with other Christians. On December 8, 1854, Pope Pius IX defined the dogma of the Immaculate Conception and gave Mary a theological significance which moved her out of the shadows of faith into the center. Although our Catholic friends assure us that Mary's sinlessness is dependent on Christ and must never be separated from his work, it is hard to keep to this because in time Mary's Immaculate Conception is prior to Christ's and in the popular mind it becomes the starting point of Christ's own mission. Instead, then, of being just the submissive agent of God's will, Mary is made an originator in her own right. So, according to Pope Pius XII's encyclical *Mystici corporis* (1943), Mary gave her consent to the spiritual marriage between the Son of God and the human race: "It was she who offered her son on Golgotha to the eternal Father. . . . It was through her prayers that the Holy Spirit was poured out upon the church at Pentecost. . . . It was she who made her son perform his first miracle." Not only are these statements exegetically incorrect, but the theology elevates Mary to a place which borders on the Godhead.

The problem is compounded further by the dogma of the bodily Assumption announced by Pius XII in 1950, which proclaims that Mary's body did not see corruption but that instead, at the end of her life, it was triumphantly taken into heaven. Taking both dogmas together, are they not in essence Christological? That is to say, Mariology seems to have become an extension of Christology because both dogmas mirror Christ's nature. He was without sin and he ascended to the Father. Now the church has attributed to his mother what the New Testament and the earliest Christian tradition made his alone.

The issue, however, cannot be limited merely to these aspects of

Christ's nature. The statements made about Mary take the problem deep into the heart of the doctrine of salvation and throw up hurdles for Christian unity. The dogmas of her Immaculate Conception and Assumption have encouraged excessive language about Mary's continuing work among Catholics. Her merits have been placed on the same level, or nearly so, as those of Christ himself, and this greatly concerns Protestants. In 1896 Leo XII called Mary the "mediatrix of the Mediator," and in 1904 Pius X spoke of Mary as the "restorer of a fallen world" and the "dispensatrix [dispenser] of all the grace Jesus won for us in his death." Benedict XV echoed these words in 1918 when he said that Mary redeemed the human race in cooperation with Christ.[1]

Protestants view this trend in Catholicism with great concern lest the heart of Christianity be blurred by applying to Mary beliefs which the New Testament affirms about Jesus Christ alone. Non-Catholics have no wish to hurl accusations at their Roman Catholic friends out of spite or to score points. On these issues we simply need assurance that the uniqueness of Jesus is not impugned.

Even though the question of Mariology remains to this day a serious obstacle to Christian unity, it is good to note progress. Over recent years greater understanding of one another's position has led to increasing convergence. Take, for example, the clarification which has come from the Catholic side. At the Second Vatican Council a significant group of Catholics wanted Mary to be elevated still higher in Catholic doctrine, even to the point of being called "co-mediator." The Council resisted the appeal of the pro-Mary lobby and made it clear that Mary's role belonged not alongside Christ's in the Godhead but within the church. Indeed, the *Dogmatic Constitution on the Church (Lumen gentium)* treads a careful middle position between the excesses of Marian devotion and a minimalism which ignores her entirely. According to section 60 her role does not obscure the "unique mediation of Christ. He is the only mediator. . . . She is at all points subordinate to Christ." Since the Council, Roman Catholic scholarship has placed an increasing emphasis on Jesus Christ, his claims and his place in the Christian life There are many helpful signs that Catholic scholars are sensitive to the problems that Mariology raises for unity with other Christians, and there is a greater willingness to face honestly the uncomfortable questions which other Christians raise.

Nevertheless at a more popular level the problem remains basically unshifted when Catholic leaders impose on Mary a structure of language and theology which is unfamiliar to other Christians and which is, in their opinion, theologically dubious. Quite often the problem intrudes innocently into areas where Catholics have every intention of being conciliatory and open to other Christians. Thus the Archbishop of Cardiff, the Most Reverend John Murphy, in his Pastoral Letter for 1983 suggests that all Christians should allow Mary to become the center of unity. She is not just a pious extra; she is an essential part of the scheme of redemption. Her feasts are not ecclesiastical embroidery or extravagant decorations of Catholic piety. They stem from one solid fact—Mary is the mother of God. The archbishop is keen to point out that Mary's role does not obscure the role of Jesus. "There is only one mediator, only one redeemer, only one head of the Mystical body, only one author of grace, Jesus Christ." But he adds, "Mary is the main distributor, the main artery, the arterial valve which assists in the circulation of that grace or as the Pope names her in the proclamation of the Jubilee, a 'mother in the order of grace.' Here then is the Marian connection: through Mary to Christ."

From a non-Catholic point of view this passage is full of stumbling blocks. Yet the archbishop seems blissfully unaware of the minefield he has laid for other Christians in his well-meaning letter.

What does it mean to see Mary as an essential part in the scheme of salvation? If the archbishop means only that she is the mother of Jesus Christ, then we are happy to affirm with him what the Scriptures say. If so, it would have helped if he had explained clearly what he meant. But he appears to be going back to the strand of theology before the Second Vatican Council which affirmed Mary's role in the order of salvation.

Furthermore, what does it mean to describe Mary as the main

distributor of grace? If the Bible gives this role to anybody, it is to the Holy Spirit. Through him the gifts and graces of God are made available to his people. But to describe Mary as the main artery of grace is foreign to the New Testament and, I would add, to the general tenor of theology for the first thousand years of the Christian church. The archbishop has just mentioned emphatically that there is only one mediator, Jesus Christ. How can we avoid the conclusion that he is now saying that Jesus has purchased our salvation, but that Mary as the main distributor of grace makes that salvation available to us? As it stands, this is a theology disagreeable to most non-Catholics, and it needs to be brought in line with the more reflective and objective style of Vatican II.

This is not to say that Protestants are faultless in their interpretation of Mary and her role. We have been inclined to go to the opposite extreme, failing to give Mary the honor given her in Scripture itself. While her figure in Scripture is shadowy, she is still "blessed among women," and the early church recognized her, along with others like Peter and Paul, as an example of faith and sacrifice, worthy of honor and respect. And having appealed to the witness of history earlier, we must listen to it here also: While Mary was not given a place in the order of salvation in the early church, she with other inspiring giants of faith were seen, not as distant historical figures, but as spiritual contemporaries whose examples were a constant inspiration and who were on hand to help in the spiritual battle of life.

On the Protestant side, the lessening of hostilities between Catholics and Protestants has allowed us to look more objectively at Mary and her place in the church. As we explore this contentious area together we may well come to common ground about Mary that will lead us into a deeper unity in Christ.

Justification by Faith—Our Deepest Difference?
Our brief look at the background to the Reformation in the previous chapter exposed the main outlines of the problem. Not only was justification by faith a serious challenge to the Catholic doctrine of salvation, but it also raised questions about the role of the sacramental

system in the order of salvation. Concerning Catholic-Protestant relationships, the first assembly of the World Council of Churches in 1948 noted that the subject of justification by faith constituted "our deepest difference."

Breakthrough. For over four hundred years the issue of justification remained a stubborn and intractable problem until Hans Küng, a young Catholic student at Tübingen University, commenced work on a Ph.D. thesis. His project was novel and daring. He set out to explore the doctrine of justification by faith, knowing that this fundamental issue separated Catholics from Protestants. His approach was to compare Catholic teaching as expressed in the canons of the Council of Trent with that of Karl Barth, the great Protestant scholar whose thought had influenced the shape of twentieth-century Christianity. Küng's published work, which was thorough and original, concluded that Catholic teaching did not in fact conflict with Barth's teaching.[2]

At first scholars on both sides were skeptical. Surely the two traditions had not been parted for over four hundred years for no solid reason at all! Barth was at first suspicious and asked Küng "whether he had arrived at this conclusion before or after he had read the Church Dogmatics"! But on investigating Küng's argument he agreed that Küng's thesis did in fact show that both traditions were surprisingly close on this important topic. How could this be true on this most crucial of doctrines? Küng pointed out that the state of war which existed in Reformation times prevented Catholics and Protestants from listening fully to one another. Views were polarized, and both sides argued from entrenched positions. "Polemics" someone has said, "is the dialog of the deaf." Unfortunately, it has been sadly true of Christian history since the sixteenth century that we have been far more anxious to talk than to listen. But, Küng argued, the passing of the age of polemics has led to a new opportunity to look afresh at the problems of the past without the weight of historical prejudice harming the dialog.[3]

Küng's own contribution took the following form:

a. Grace is primary. The priority of grace is often thought to be a Protestant emphasis. But Küng's analysis of Trent and Barth's theology revealed unanimity on the fact that grace precedes everything in the Christian life. Without God we can do nothing. We have no intrinsic goodness to save ourselves; salvation is a free gift of God. The Council of Trent was just as fierce as the Reformers in denouncing good deeds as the basis of salvation; without grace our actions have no value.[4] Indeed, comments Küng, the irony of the sixteenth century was that both the Reformers and the Tridentine fathers accused each other of Pelagianism, that is, teaching that human goodness has merit in God's sight for salvation. According to Catholics, Protestants appeared to make faith a giant work in which they trusted for salvation; furthermore, they seemed to deny the importance of good deeds as well as the role of the church. A subjective faith appeared to be the center of Protestantism. On the other hand, according to Protestants, Catholics appeared to be preaching that salvation depended on living a moral life and performing religious duties, instead of trusting in a Savior who had already purchased our redemption. Küng therefore showed that Catholics and Protestants agree that God's grace, which excludes all human boasting, is the basis of everything in the Christian life.

b. *Justification is not a process but a declaration about a relationship.* As we saw earlier, Catholics at the time of the Reformation had followed Augustine in making justification a process of salvation. They had therefore blurred the distinction between justification and sanctification. Not unreasonably on their terms—which saw salvation as an ongoing process in the life of the Christian, fed from the confluence of the church's ministry and the individual's life of faith—they accused Protestants of ignoring the demands of holiness. Küng acknowledges that many of the theological difficulties of the sixteenth century could have been avoided if Catholic scholars had paid more careful attention to the meaning of the word *justify* in the New Testament, instead of following Augustine's interpretation that it means "to *make* righteous." Küng points out that the verb is a legal term; it simply states that the accused is acquitted, not that he is made righteous. Küng's understanding of what Protestants were trying to say about the nature of justification is therefore very significant, because he sees that they were not trying to deny the importance of the Christian life but attempting to show that Christianity is essentially about a relationship with Jesus Christ. Becoming righteous is not the basis of salvation, because there is only one basis, the salvation offered to each of us through Christ. Justification is simply God's declaration that "because of the death and resurrection of Jesus Christ, the person who believes the Gospel is in the right."[5]

  c. *The Christian is sinful and righteous.* Küng also showed that the Reformers' argument that a Christian is at one and the same time sinful and righteous has always been Catholic teaching. Unfortunately at the Reformation the famous phrase *simul justus et peccator* seemed to suggest to Catholics that justification was a legal fiction because it made no difference to Christians. It left them where they were, weak and in their sin. On the other hand, Catholics insisted, Catholic teaching emphasized a real restitution of sinners by which they are made children and heirs of promise. It was extraordinary, indeed, how this simple phrase was open to such confusing interpretations. Luther intended it to clarify the theology that in Christ we are righteous while in ourselves we are sinful and helpless. He did not intend the phrase to suggest that Christians had a schizoid nature, or that Christians were not in any real sense children of God, or that Christianity made no difference to the way believers lived. Küng made the issues clear and showed substantial areas of agreement.

  Post-Küng Research. Since Küng's important book Catholic scholarship has continued in this field of study, and as a result considerable theological convergence has come about. As Tony Lane notes, "The effect of Küng's book has been a widespread feeling among Roman Catholic theologians that the doctrine of justification by faith alone is acceptable and need not divide the confessions. Since the Roman Catholic Church reinterprets its faith as it goes along, this fact is at least as significant as the theoretical question of whether or not the doctrines are really compatible."[6] We might go even further. Isn't it more important that many Roman Catholic theologians today agree with the Protestant understanding of justification than whether they rightly or wrongly believe their view can be squared with that of Trent? In any case, let us look briefly at three aspects of the doctrine of justification where Catholics and Protestants have built on Küng's foundations.

a. Faith and love. As we have seen, Catholics at the Reformation argued that justification by faith seemed to make no difference to human hearts and beliefs. Luther and the other Reformers strongly denied this, but the notion that the Protestant faith was an external thing stuck. Today Catholic theologians stoutly defend Luther from such criticism. "For Luther faith is something alive and active. . . . Faith cannot exist without love and good works."[7] It is, as we know, good Protestant doctrine to assert that when people come to believe in Christ the outworking of their newfound faith is in a worthy life, because they are now under the direction of a new master. Just as fruit is the proof of a living fruit tree so the proof of faith is a worthy life. Works, therefore, cannot be divorced from faith; they go hand in glove with it.

b. Made right with God. Küng is not a lone Catholic voice crying in the wastes of Catholic sacramentalism. Volk, for example, states that "the idea of imputation [that is, that the sinner is clothed with Christ's righteousness] and thus the forensic dimension cannot be dropped."[8] Michael Schmaus, a prominent Catholic theologian, also commends the insights of the Reformers: "The Reformers teach that God truly punishes sin. If then God declares the sinner justified, he is made wholly just."[9] Harding Meyer sums up the present state of scholarship on this subject: "The Reformation doctrine of justification has had for some time an important and increasing number of Catholic advocates. Catholic theologians seem nowadays to have relieved their Protestant colleagues from the worry of having to justify the doctrine of justification."[10] Such steady agreement on the character of justification as being made right with God is a most important convergence and a cause of some rejoicing.

c. Merit and salvation. If Catholics need to be convinced that Protestants believe in the importance of good living and good deeds, Protestants need to be convinced that Catholics do not believe they can merit their salvation. From one point of view the doctrine of merit is extremely strange because the Council of Trent emphatically denied the value of human action in appropriating God's approval. As we have seen, a consistent note in the Council was the primacy of grace. It insisted that the "efficient cause of justification is the merciful God who freely washes and sanctifies us." "Nothing precedes justification," it says, "nothing merits the grace of justification, . . . otherwise grace is no longer grace." Furthermore, "a Christian should have no need to rely on himself or to glory in himself, instead of the Lord whose goodness towards all men is that he wants *his gifts to be their merits*."[11] The last phrase is taken from Augustine, who saw everything in the Christian life as flowing from grace.

So then, why is it that in spite of Trent's strong insistence on the impossibility of human goodness earning God's approval, there has been such a fondness for merit in Catholicism?

Part of the answer must lie in the fact that the Council of Trent was in itself an act of reform. The Fathers of the Council realized that on many issues the Reformers rightly reacted against the corruption of medieval religion. Medieval Christianity was dominated by the concept of the value of human activity. The prominence of indulgences reflected such belief. Although the canons of Trent represent an important theological attack on Pelagianism, they never really penetrated to rank-and-file Catholicism.

To this day there has been a penchant for making salvation a process which requires our constant good deeds and works of love to keep us in the faith. Statements from bishops and church leaders offer the faithful blessings if certain duties are done. For example, to return to the Archbishop of Cardiff's 1983 Pastoral Letter, the archbishop exhorts his flock: "In this Jubilee of the Redemption extra graces abound. A renewed devotion to Mary, a daily rosary, a week-day Mass, a Deanery Mass, the statues of the cross can produce for you and for non-Catholic friends a greater share in these graces. Start immediately this Lent."

Clearly here is an understanding of grace depicted like a treasury which is enlarged through religious duties. It is a heavenly bank which accumulates our earthly credit. Now few would deny the value or the importance of such acts, but the picture of faith which emerges from this is that of the Christian life built on meritorious deeds rather than on a loving response to Christ. Human activity has come to be seen as the root of grace rather than as its fruit. The portrayal of grace by the archbishop is that of merit flowing from us to God rather than from God to us. Perhaps that is not the archbishop's intention, but that appears to be the natural inference from his thought.

The other factor at the heart of this problem we will put as a question: What, in fact, is the real value of merit? We must acknowledge that the term *merit* has had a long history in the Christian church. Tertullian, a third-century theologian, was the first to employ this word to denote our response to God's action in Christ. He had been trained as a lawyer, and his terminology has had a lasting effect on theological vocabulary, notably on the doctrine of God. But the idea of merit was not his best contribution to theology because it was a wrong interpretation of the New Testament word *reward*.[12] When Jesus spoke about reward, he was not referring to our claim on God but to our response to his claims on us. The Scriptures are emphatic that Jesus Christ is the only foundation and that faith in him is the only door. But again and again Jesus reminded his disciples that morality is at the heart of the faith and not outside it. The man who buries his talents does not receive a reward; he is a disobedient and faithless servant. Paul reinforces this in 1 Corinthians 3 where he teaches that on the one foundation of Jesus Christ various buildings can be erected—gold, silver, hay and so forth—and that the final day will reveal the character of the life lived. In other words, good works have an eschatological reference; they will receive a reward in heaven. We are not saved by such works—Paul has already made that clear—but in some undefined way God's approval awaits those who honor him. So the Augsburg Confession suggests: "Upon good works depends the difference between the saints in glory."

Tertullian's mistake was to transfer reward from its eschatological perspective to that of salvation, thus making the Christian life dependent on the character of our lives instead of active faith in Christ. Thus, followed to its logical end, such thinking makes the church a kind of glorified spiritual shop in which our deeds are presented in exchange for the promise of future blessings.

Many present-day Catholic theologians are just as severe in their denounciation of this concept of merit as Protestants are. Karl Rahner points out that grace and merit are contradictions in terms. If God's grace is at the heart of salvation and every human act, the idea of merit in this context is entirely unwarranted. If merit is to have any meaning, he continues, it must refer to the "dynamic quality of human existence in which grace meets with our response issuing in love and obedience."[13] Otto Pesch, a Catholic theologian, pleads for a new terminology to express more precisely what we mean. The term *merit,* he points out, not only conjures up wrongly the idea of what we do to claim God's approval, but it is also tarnished with the disputes of a bygone age.[14] It might well be better to return to the biblical category of reward.

Justification—The Leaven Which Makes the Dough Rise. It is heartening that many Catholic and Protestant theologians have discovered such unity on what has long been seen as our deepest difference. This is a remarkable breakthrough and encourages us to believe that if common perceptions can be arrived at on such a major issue, there is hope that agreement can be reached elsewhere.[15]

However, in case it should be thought that justification by faith is a mere evangelical "bee in the bonnet," we should make clear that this doctrine has repercussions for many other aspects of Christian theology. As Luther suggests, justification is the leaven which makes the dough rise.

For example, it affects our understanding of the ministry and the sacraments of the church. As we have already observed, not only did the Reformation doctrine of justification challenge the idea of justification on the basis of human merit, but it also indirectly attacked a sacramental system which was considered to be the channel of God's saving graces. Evangelicals have no wish to strip away ornate styles of celebration or to replace beauty and dignity in worship by plainness and dullness. We can learn much from the Catholic emphasis on color, reverence, beauty and order. But the issue is that the sacraments of the church should be brought in line with our understanding of the character of faith. Justification by faith declares to our hearts: "You are ransomed, healed, restored, forgiven. You are brought near to God through Christ, and you are made a member of his family."

The sacrament of Holy Communion or the Mass should express this. If it declares a different doctrine, that through the sacrament we are restored to God, then it undermines the doctrine of justification. The Eucharist is not a *means* of salvation but an *expression* of it. It declares the finished work of Christ to which we can add nothing. This does not limit or weaken Holy Communion itself. The Eucharist remains the focal point of Christian worship because it commemorates the saving activity of Christ on the cross. As we feed on him by faith, his grace is made available to us for daily living and strength.

The same principle holds for ministry as well. In the Medieval Period the concept of ministry had shrunk to the notion of priesthood. The be-all and end-all of ministry was the sacramental priesthood in which the priest represented man to God and God to man. He stood between as an intermediary, a channel through which God's grace came. But justification by faith rests on the unique priesthood and mediatorship of Christ and never in the same sense on human mediation or Christian ministry. All we can do is to point to his perfect ministry and priesthood and rejoice in the benefits which flow from them. Justification, therefore, declares the finished work of the cross and leads to the rediscovery of the essentials of Christian ministry: proclamation and pastoral oversight, as well as the celebration of the Eucharist.

The Bible and Tradition
The aim of the Reformation was the renewal of the whole church.

Luther had no intention initially to break away from the Catholic Church. He wanted to restore the church to its original purity as expressed in Scripture. From this point of view the "reformation" was unsuccessful in that it led to further fragmentation of the Christian church, the sixteenth-century division of the Western churches adding to the schism of Orthodox and Catholic churches which took place in 1054.

In the long run, however, the Reformation had its positive effect on the Roman Catholic Church. It led to Catholic reform, one of its chief expressions being the Council of Trent which convened April 8, 1546. The Council dealt with many issues, but, in addition to the more obvious corrections that were required, the Council had to respond to the central plank of the Reformation—the primacy of Scripture. The question of the authority of the Bible became therefore a key theological issue of the day.

The Reformers asserted that Scripture alone (sola scriptura) was the basis of doctrine: all ecclesiastical practices should be tested and judged in the light of Scripture. The Council of Trent retorted that the source of Christian teaching is not only the Bible but also the oral traditions of the church. "The sacred Council of Trent observe that the sacred saving truth and moral teaching of the Gospel is contained in written books and in the unwritten traditions of Christ himself." By the "unwritten traditions of Christ" they meant the teaching and practices of the church, which they assumed must have come from Christ in the first place. Scripture and oral tradition are to be received with the same degree of love and affection. Revelation is found partly in Scripture and partly in tradition. So the two-source theory began.[16]

Josef Geiselmann, a leading Roman Catholic theologian, argues, however, that Trent did not decide the issue of the relationship between the Bible and tradition definitively: "Nothing, absolutely nothing was decided at the Council of Trent concerning the relation of Scripture and tradition." There was so much confusion at Trent, he maintains, that the Council left the matter unresolved. "God is no plumber. He does not provide the church with running water, letting the Word of God flow out of two sources of faith, Scripture and tradition, as out of two taps marked hot and cold."[17]

Whether Geiselmann is correct or not is a matter of debate. In any event, whether it was the Council's intent or not, it encouraged a two-source idea of revelation which has prevailed within Catholicism such that the Bible and tradition have been treated as independent means of revelation. Statements of truth gathered from tradition have been held to be revealed even though they lack any confirmation from Scripture.

Here the matter rested until the Second Vatican Council took up the issue. The first significant thing that happened was that the two-source concept of revelation, at least as expressed at Trent, was rejected. An earlier draft prepared for the Council separated the Bible and tradition as two sources of revelation.[18] The Council, however, affirmed that revelation is "God revealing *himself* (not just doctrines) through deeds and words."[19] That revelation finds its fullest expression in Jesus Christ, the Word of God, from whom flow both sacred Scripture and sacred tradition:

This plan of revelation is realized by deeds and words having an inner unity: the deeds wrought by God in the history of salvation manifest and confirm the teaching and realities signified by the words, while the words proclaim the deeds and clarify the mystery contained in them. By this revelation then, the deepest truth about God and the salvation of man is made clear to us in Christ, who is the Mediator and at the same time the fullness of all revelation.[20]

Protestants might ask whether the Council's rejection of the two-source concept of revelation in favor of the one-source concept makes any practical difference. After all, both concepts seem to place Scripture and sacred tradition on the same level. What is clear, however, is that the Council viewed the Bible as central to Christian theology and life. In *Dei verbum* the Council proclaimed that the written Word of God "is the soul of sacred theology, and because of this the clergy are encouraged to study the Bible and make it the center of their spiritual lives. For ignorance of Scripture is ignorance of Christ."[21]

This call for a greater commitment to a faith grounded in Scripture is one of the great achievements of Vatican II. With that encouragement Catholic scholars have studied the Bible with fresh vigor, and in recent years some of the most exciting developments in biblical studies have come from Catholics. At a more popular level, over the last fifteen years Bible study among Catholics has flourished. More and more Catholic churches have developed Bible study groups, thus allowing the Bible to shape them.

But skeptics will ask, "Have Catholics and Protestants really come to agree about the authority of Scripture? Even if we grant that the Vatican II statement is a step in the right direction from a Protestant perspective, is it adequate to settle the dispute over the role of tradition in theology?"

It is important to recognize that the dispute here is not over the authority of the Bible per se. Official Catholic teaching shares with evangelical Protestants a high view of Scripture, recognizing its divine inspiration and authoritative witness to Christ. Scripture, Catholics maintain, is the *"norma normans non normata"* (the standard for all other norms which is not itself subject to a greater norm).[22] The dispute lies over the place to be given the church in interpreting the Bible and in supplementing its teaching.

Protestants have held that the Bible is self-interpreting under the illumination of the Holy Spirit. Catholics, however, reject what they call "private interpretation," arguing instead that the church is the proper interpreter of Scripture. Oddly enough, on this issue there has always been much greater agreement than Protestants have been willing to admit. Protestants do not hesitate to speak of historic Christianity, by which they mean those doctrines which are expressed in the great councils and creeds of Christendom. Both Protestants and Catholics look back to these councils and creeds for an understanding of the person of Christ and the nature of the Godhead. Throughout church history there have been those who have denied these formulations of the faith, claiming to base their understanding on Scripture alone. Yet such private interpretations have never gained the status of orthodoxy. Thus even for Protestants there is a sense in which the church defines what an orthodox and what a heretical understanding of Scripture is.

Part of the problem here rests on a common Protestant misunderstanding of the Catholic teaching office, the magisterium. Even the term *magisterium* conjures up in the minds of many Protestants a select group of men arbitrarily declaring the church's teaching on a wide variety of issues. The magisterium is not a small, fixed body. Rather it is a large, fluid one, embracing the Pope and bishops by reason of their office and Catholic theologians by reason of their scholarly competence. Thus the magisterium functions much like respected pastors, teachers and scholars within Protestantism.

An issue of more serious dispute lies over the ability of the church to require assent to doctrine that cannot be proved from Scripture. Protestants have always rejected this. Catholics maintain that tradition as "the living and lived faith of the Church" may also require assent even when it is not directly grounded in Scripture.[23] If a dogma is authenticated by the teaching office of the church (the magisterium), regardless of whether it has a base in Scripture, it is to be believed. If it is to be believed, it must be scriptural. In this seemingly circular scheme, tradition/Scripture/magisterium form a tight defensive system that protects Catholic theology from criticism.

Here Catholics might learn from Protestants. If the church itself decides what is to be believed, where does the uniqueness of Scripture lie? In what way is it normative for faith? In areas of faith where the Bible is silent, are we justified in raising certain beliefs to the level of dogma binding on all Christians? How can Scripture ever reform the church in this system?

Roman Catholics object further to the Protestant idea of *sola scriptura*, pointing out (1) that the church defined the canon of Scripture and (2) that Scripture itself is a form of tradition. Both these points should be taken seriously by Protestants and weighed carefully.

Protestants all too easily cry *sola scriptura* without acknowledging that apart from the church we would not have the book we call the Bible. Apart from the church there would be no well-defined canon. After all, nowhere in the Bible as we know it is there any list telling us which individual books belong within its covers.

Historically the formation of the canon took place in response to heresy. During the second century the church was pressured to decide which books it would acknowledge as authoritative. But the argument here cuts both ways. True enough, as Catholics have argued, it was the church that defined the canon, and Protestants have not often appreciated the significance of the Christian community in that process. Yet, on the other hand, Catholics have sometimes given the impression that in bringing forth the canon the church was proclaiming its own authority rather than recognizing the authority inherent in the books themselves as part of God's self-revelation.

Looking into the principal criterion by which books were included in or excluded from the New Testament canon only increases our sense of the tension between the roles of tradition and inherent authority. The key issue was apostolicity. Did the book in question come directly from the hand of an apostle or at least from a close associate with apostolic approval? If so, the book was accepted. If not, it wasn't. But was this because the apostles represented the teaching office of the church, or because they were uniquely inspired to produce the New Testament canon?

Protestants and Catholics would probably want to join together in affirming both reasons. Catholics, however, would emphasize the first and argue that the teaching office of the apostles continues within the church through its bishops. Protestants, on the other hand, would stress the second and argue that, because the canon is now complete, apostolic authority resides within it and it should stand over all human authority within the church.

On any reading, however, the apostles' teaching clearly preceded not only the definition of the canon but the writing of the New Testament documents themselves. And here Catholics offer another just criticism of Protestants. Protestants, they claim, seldom appreciate the degree to which the New Testament itself incorporates and formalizes tradition. The Gospel accounts of Jesus' death and resurrection especially, as well as hymns such as those found in Philippians 2:6-11 and Ephesians 5:14, undoubtedly circulated widely through oral tradition and were used in corporate worship before they were ever included in Scripture. Thus Scripture and tradition are much more interconnected than Protestants sometimes seem willing to admit.

Nevertheless, we must not lose sight of the primacy of the apostolic witness as recorded in Scripture. As Catholic theologian Gerald O'Collins writes in *Fundamental Theology:* "Through the inspired record of their foundational and constitutive experience, preaching and action, the members of the apostolic church remain uniquely authoritative for all subsequent generations of Christians. Thus the priority of that apostolic church was and is much more than a temporary one."[24] In other words, the authority of the New Testament is basic to the later church because it is the inspired record of God's action in the church.

This leads into another area where Catholics and Protestants have differed—the relationship between the first generation of Christians and the later church. If we make the Bible so special, Catholics argue, are we not in danger of separating the Bible from the church? The New Testament is the first layer of the church's tradition, the record of first-century faith.

But it is one thing to recognize that Scripture derives in part from tradition and quite another to conclude that other traditions are on a par with it. As the apostolic witness to Christ, the New Testament is unique and therefore normative for all other traditions. What the first Christians believed and taught about Christ is authoritatively more important than, say, the teaching of St. Teresa of Ávila or Martin Luther. This is because they were primary witnesses of God's action in Christ and were called by the Holy Spirit to write about it.

Even though Catholics and Protestants still have some way to go before they agree on the relationship between the Bible and tradition, there are heartening signs of agreement. The fact that Catholic theology has moved away from a rigid two-source idea of revelation, which kept Scripture and tradition apart, is an important development. Scripture now has a central place in the church's discovery of God's will.

Protestants too have grown in their understanding of the Bible. Having long seen the Scriptures as somehow distinct from the church, they are beginning to see the Bible as the church's book as well as God's. There is an interaction between the Bible and the church which is deep and God-given. The church reveres and protects the Scriptures and yet at the same time places itself under the divine scrutiny of God's Word. While the New Testament is rightly seen as growing from tradition, it is nevertheless that part of tradition which governs all that follows. It is the yardstick by which all else is tested. To treat Scripture as but the beginning of the development of theology, or as the junior partner of tradition, is to step onto the slippery slope of relativism, because the criterion of truth passes from the testimony of Scripture to that of authorities within the church.

Whether we are Catholic or Protestant we recognize that many of the questions the Reformation raised about the Bible are still with us. We have much yet to resolve. In the *Final Report* of the Anglican-Roman Catholic International Commission (1982), the theologians representing both sides wrote, "The person and work of Jesus Christ, preached by the apostles and set forth and interpreted as the New Testament writings, through the inspiration of the Holy Spirit, are the primary norm for Christian faith and life. . . . Since the Scriptures are the uniquely inspired witness to divine revelation, the church's expression of that revelation must be tested by its consonance with Scripture."[25]

Such a statement is a sign of hope. If it were truly possible for both traditions to work from this base, we might well arrive on common ground.

Chapter 4
COMMON
RESERVOIR

*W*e saw earlier that one of the unfortunate results of the Reformation was a divided Christendom. From the Reformation on, Catholics and Protestants drifted steadily apart, each separately claiming Christian truth and denying it to the other. Almost total separation followed the bitterness of the sixteenth century. The long silence began. Even today, despite attempts to bring us together, many on both sides believe that the differences are too great to bridge.

A friend of mine, visiting in London with a group of Protestants, was astonished to hear the vitriol uttered against the Roman Catholic Church: Corrupt, evil, unbiblical, impure, unfaithful, apostate. These descriptions just did not tally with his experience of meeting many lovely Catholic Christians whose faith in Christ was as deep and as real as his own. He found himself asking why a so-called corrupt church produced such devout and dedicated Christians.

Then again, a Roman Catholic friend told me that she was brought up to regard all Protestants with suspicion and fear. Her parish priest taught that the Protestant churches had deviated from the truth of Catholicism: their spirituality was impoverished, their doctrine distorted, their teaching deficient. When she met Protestants for the first time at university, she wondered how such sincere, Bible-believing Christians could be so far from the truth!

The truth is that we are not as far apart as some people make out. Many significant differences and daunting problems block the way ahead as we have observed, but significant points of agreement show that we are not talking about two distinct religions trying to come together. We are actually sister churches which belong together, bound by common beliefs. Or, to change the metaphor, we are like an estranged married couple who discover on encountering one another by accident that they cannot throw away the past. As they meet and talk, aware of all the bitterness and misunderstanding that has driven them apart, they realize with perhaps some surprise that more unites than separates them. But my contention needs some explanation because not all Protestants are inclined to believe that the Roman Catholic Church is in *any* sense a true church, and not all Roman Catholics are likely to believe that truth can be discovered outside the Roman fold. Here are some factors which indicate that we draw from a common reservoir.[1]

The Reality of God
In February 1982 a lovely event in Newcastle, England, made the headlines in some of our national papers. A brother and sister met for the first time after forty years of separation. Their family had been captured by the Nazis and sent to different concentration camps. When the war ended only the two survived, although neither knew that the other still lived. The brother eventually came to England, and the sister went to the States. Years passed, and then one day through another relation they were reunited. As the papers recounted, the two found that, in spite of the many years apart and their separate cultural development, nothing could alter the fact that they belonged together in a special way.

Christians have that experience as they talk about God. As they talk they discover those family roots which not only join them but separate them from others.

Two contrasting examples might help explain what I mean. When I was in the Royal Air Force doing my national service, the Christian fellowship I attended used to have an open Bible study and discussion group. It came as quite a jolt to us all one evening, as we shared our experience of the fatherhood of God, to realize that we represented eight different denominations, including Roman Catholicism. Yet, somehow, our church allegiance, important though it was, did not matter. What was of greater importance was our common starting point in having a relationship with God. We belonged to one another through him.

The second, and totally different, experience which springs to mind was a recent course I taught in my church. One of our leaders brought along a Muslim who was interested in Christianity. Our subject was Jesus, and we had a most fascinating discussion about him. But what emerged was a different understanding of God. The New Testament notion of God as a father who cares and who enters into human affairs by sending his son Jesus to die for us was completely mystifying to our Muslim friend. Through no fault of our own his understanding of God removed him from the Christian family.

Here, then, is a common starting point of some importance among Christians—the reality of God. A God who is known in Jesus Christ and experienced through the Holy Spirit. This is at the heart of both Catholic and Protestant confessions of faith.

But what kind of faith in God is this, and how do we know it represents real unity? The suspicion that lingers here is similar to that which exists between an estranged couple who say to one another "I love you" but wonder if the other means it. Somehow words and actions must fit together.

In our statements about God's nature we do indeed say very similar things. Catholics and Protestants are equally emphatic about God as a loving, heavenly father. By this we mean more than just that God is like a human father. The word *father* is not merely analogical; it means that God has revealed himself as father of all. It is his nature to express this fatherhood in his providential care of all who love him. Christians of all traditions believe that God has chosen to reveal himself in this way and that he may be discovered as such. When St. Augustine became a Christian in the fourth century, his understanding of God was revolutionized. That abstract being, which up to then had been a subject of philosophical inquiry, was now a person as real as himself and closer than the dearest love he had known.

But the peculiarity of the Christian God is that he is only really known through Jesus Christ. The fellow who once said "I am a God-the-Father kind of Christian" *may* have been uttering a profound remark, but it would not have been understood by New Testament Christians. Only through Jesus is God known as father. An essay by Karl Rahner notes that Ignatius of Loyola once said, "The Christianity which can bypass Jesus to find the incomprehensible God does not exist. God has willed that many, unutterably many, should find Jesus simply because they seek him."[2]

Modern theologians who try to make Christianity more accessible by reducing Jesus to the level of a good example or an amazing, charismatic human figure actually make God more inaccessible because, as Paul put it, "Christ is the image of the invisible God." And Jesus himself is at the heart of our agreement as Christians. There is no squabble here. He is the divine Son of God who has brought to mankind a full and lasting salvation. It is indeed true that differences have arisen about how that salvation is experienced and how Jesus Christ is known, but orthodox Catholics and Protestants are one in believing in the finality of Jesus Christ for human existence. It was not a Protestant but St. Teresa of Ávila, no less, who once said, "All the way to heaven is heaven, because Jesus said 'I am the way.'"

It is a sad commentary on modern ecumenism that instead of beginning with primary questions of faith—such as the centrality of Jesus, the nature of faith, the issue of discipleship—we tend to allow other issues to overshadow such basic matters. In the Gospels Jesus did not ask his disciples "What do you think about realized eschatology?" or "What precisely are your beliefs about God?" He asked, "Who do you say I am?" That is, belief in him is the heart of the Christian faith, and he is the center of the church.

In a terse and pithy statement St. Augustine described the nature of the church: *"Ubi Christus, ibi ecclesia"* ("Where Christ is, there is the church"). That is, where there is a sincere and lively faith in Christ, the Son of God, there is the church of Jesus.

It is a pity that ecumenical discussions concentrate almost totally on major areas of difference instead of spending time considering the areas of theology where we already agree. Protestants and Catholics have the same devotion to Christ. He is the risen Lord, the only Mediator and Savior. We chant the same creeds about Christ, and we acknowledge that belief in his full humanity and divinity is the bedrock of Christianity. Yet, somehow, this common focus is overlooked.

New Testament faith suggests that when each of us faces the Great Judge, we shall not be asked "What church did you belong to?" but "How did you respond to the call and claims of Jesus Christ? Did you follow him through life as your Lord and model? Were his standards yours?"

We also share a common emphasis on the Holy Spirit as the giver of life to the church and to the Christian. From the Scriptures we draw the same teaching that God the Holy Spirit is given to his people for life, for growth and for mission. Protestants have no quibble with Catholic emphasis on the Spirit as source of the church's life; and, as far as I am aware, neither have Catholics any objection to the teaching from the Protestant direction that the Spirit indwells people. Perspectives differ nonetheless, Catholics more likely emphasizing the Spirit's indwelling of structures and Protestants more likely stressing the Spirit's extraordinary ministry outside structures. Yet both agree that it would be sub-Christian to ignore the Spirit completely.

In recent years many denominations have remarkably come together through charismatic renewal. This renewal has come about, partly at least, through a rediscovery of the biblical doctrine of the Spirit. The Anglican Bishop of Winchester, John Taylor, in *The Go-Between God,* comments on the need for doctrine and experience to be one: "While we proudly respect the traditional assertion that without the Holy Spirit we can get nowhere in the Christian mission, we seem to press on notwithstanding with our man-made programmes. I have not heard recently of committee business adjourned because those present were still awaiting the Spirit of God. I have known projects abandoned for lack of funds, but not for lack of the gifts of the Spirit."[3]

These days, however, churches are likely to pay more than passing attention to the Holy Spirit. Charismatic renewal has brought home to Christians the fact that the Spirit is not merely a theological abstraction but the life-giving power of God. I remember attending a charismatic meeting in the Gregorian University in Rome in February 1976. I was taken along by a friend who thought I would be interested in discovering another aspect of Catholicism. About four hundred people were present, the vast majority Roman Catholic. Charismatic songs were sung with verve, there were speaking in tongues, singing in the Spirit and other expressions of charismatic worship. But what impressed me most was the openness of the meeting as Christians of all denominations met in the Spirit, in the Lord. It was a truly ecumenical meeting because we were united in Christ. In that act of worship we were embraced by a unity given by the Spirit.

That meeting in which we were able to unite so freely in Christ and share in the gifts of his Spirit stands in sad contrast to the divisions which keep Christians apart. And yet in hope we can grasp such opportunities for shared worship as a foreshadowing of the unity which we trust will be ours one day.

Cardinal Suenens, one of the most significant Catholic leaders at the Second Vatican Council and a leader of Catholic charismatic renewal, once wrote: "We must have a living, serene faith in the Holy Spirit working as well as within the church, yesterday, today and tomorrow." Of course he was right. Without the Holy Spirit the church is but a human institution struggling to find a future; with him it becomes a divine fellowship, vibrant with new life and fresh possibilities. Cardinal Suenens was once asked why he was a man of hope. He replied: "I am an optimist because I believe that the Holy Spirit is the Spirit of creation. To those who welcome him he gives each day fresh freedom and a renewal of joy and hope."[4] With the Spirit of Jesus we surely find strong ground for believing that God can draw us together.

The Word of God

Earlier we glanced at our different approaches to Scripture and its authority, and we rightly observed that on questions of interpretation there is still progress to be made. Nevertheless, we do share a similar attitude to the Bible in seeing it as having a unique place in the life of the church and the Christian. Catholics and Protestants find themselves agreeing not only that God has spoken in the past but that he continues to speak today. The primary vehicle he has chosen to use is the Scriptures, which are for us all God's Word.

One trap we must not fall into is to assume that the Bible is exclusively God's Word as if he speaks in no other way. This would, in fact, restrict the biblical concept of the word which, in the Old Testament, is used of God's action in creation and salvation and, in the New Testament, finds its definitive expression in Jesus who entered human existence to make God known. He is God's Word par excellence. Nevertheless, Catholics and Protestants find it possible to talk of the Bible as God's Word because of its unique, divine inspiration and the record it gives us of the saving activity and ministry of Jesus. It is the written testament of God's covenant with us, conveying his expressed will concerning his gift of salvation to all. It is therefore something quite unique, special and authoritative. The church has always recognized this. When the church produced a canon of Scripture in the period after the New Testament, it was declaring that primarily in these books do we find the authority for our life, teaching and witness.

Here we might discover a partial answer to the old question "which came first, the church or the Bible?" This used to be a popular debating point between Protestants and Catholics.

Protestants were apt to make the Bible the basis for everything while Catholics asserted the primacy of the church's teaching. We are more likely these days to say, "Well, we can't quite put it like that because the gospel itself preceded both and gave birth to the Bible and the church." The message written down in the New Testament books was the very gospel which, through God's Spirit, created the church. The writings of the Old and New Testaments, therefore, undoubtedly shaped the small Christian community in the first century.

On the other hand, the church under the Holy Spirit had an important role in deciding which books were included in the canon of Scripture. Thus, the church *recognized* what, in fact, brought it into being and, by recognizing the authority of certain books, anchored its faith deeply and firmly in the apostolic church of the New Testament.

The impact of Jesus and his gospel of freedom, in other words, gave simultaneous birth to what we might call twins, the fellowship of believers and the apostolic writings. Ignore one of the two, or exaggerate one at the expense of the other, and you end up with a deficient Christianity. For example, if I say "The Bible is sufficient; I don't need Christian fellowship," I end in an individualism which Catholics used to term "the Protestant heresy." If, on the other hand, I say "The church is all-sufficient; I can ignore what Scripture teaches," I will be cutting myself off from the roots of the faith, for how can I possibly verify the truth of what the church teaches unless I check it against the Bible?

One of the blessings of the modern age is that as Christians from different churches have come into contact with each other, we have discovered that the Bible is the major thing we have in common. It is our ecumenical nexus. We lay claim to it as our final authority, and it is at the heart of our worship. Hans Küng, the well-known and controversial Catholic theologian, says of the importance of the Bible for Catholics, "Scripture is the well from which Catholic doctrine and Catholic theology draws the Word of God. The Word of God in the strictest sense is sacred Scripture alone. Scripture thus has an absolute precedence which no theological argument can whittle away."[5]

While, then, Scripture is at the center of Catholic and Protestant faith and worship, we must reiterate the point made in the previous chapter that it is one thing to affirm the priority of Scripture and another to interpret it. Although the Second Vatican Council moved a long way from the rigid two-source theory of revelation as propounded by the Council of Trent, it did not, as we observed, clearly distinguish the respective roles of Bible and tradition. In a sophisticated theological explanation it speaks of one source of divine revelation expressed in two modes of transmission. Christ is the source of revelation, and the two forms in which revelation is communicated to us are the Bible and tradition, "sacred tradition and sacred Scripture forming one sacred deposit of the Word of God."[6]

Furthermore, the task of interpreting the Word has been entrusted *exclusively* to the living teaching office of the church. As we pointed out earlier, this interpretation makes Catholic doctrine well-nigh impregnable. Even if a dogma has dubious scriptural warrant, Catholics are content to trust the magisterium that the dogma has sufficient support in the received traditions of the church.

Protestants also take their starting point in the lordship of Christ, the revealer of truth. Living under his leadership and guidance, Protestants believe that the church must base its teaching, morals and worship on the written Word of God. The Bible must have priority over all other authorities. All doctrines and received traditions must be checked and tested in the light of Scripture. Nothing can stand independent of it, whatever church leaders might say, because the church has no right to add to what Scripture declares.

Are we then forced to conclude that the way we take the Bible as our authority constitutes an unbridgeable gulf? By no means. If the Bible is at the heart of our faith, it is therefore a potential bridge to unity, and we should allow it to address us freely.

While it is obvious that Protestants and Catholics have not yet reached full agreement on how Scripture should function within the church, Protestants should take heart that the same dogmatic constitution that urges the faithful to be diligent in reading Scripture also encourages the clergy to preach and teach it. Since the Council, Catholic Christians have increased in their love of the Scripture and in their desire to be more Bible-based. We need not fear the future or lose hope if Christians, Protestants as well as Catholics, allow the Scriptures to irrigate the channels of spiritual life.

The Church
At first sight everything appears to separate Catholic from Protestant

when the word *church* is mentioned. It seems inconceivable that we shall find any room for encouragement here. "Two different worlds," we might think when we compare the ritualism of Rome with the informal practices of most of Protestantism.

But the church is important to all Christians, even though certain elements of the doctrine of the church, or *ecclesiology* as it is called, may have different significance for us. Catholics stress the notion of the visible church, the body of Christ in society. They point proudly to the unity of that fellowship—the Catholic Church in Amsterdam, Paris, Buenos Aires and San Francisco and so on—a unity which transcends language and culture. They also emphasize the hierarchical nature of the church anchored in its episcopacy centering in the papal office.

Protestants likewise have a doctrine of the church that is important for them. To be sure, because Protestantism comprises many different fellowships, there are many differing attitudes to the visible fellowship. Some Protestants, especially those in Anglican and Lutheran churches, hold views similar to those of Roman Catholics, granting greater attention to the visible church with its rites and ceremonies. Others, however, pay less attention to the hierarchical church, preferring to stress the spiritual unity of all believers, arguing that obedience to Jesus as head is the real test of belonging to Christ's body. While they do not deny the importance of the visible congregation of Christians, they attach greater significance to personal commitment, which they believe is the true bond between believers and Christ and which simultaneously binds them to all other Christians.

In these two attitudes, I want to suggest, lies a common element of sacramentality which is at the heart of our commitment to that unworthy fellowship of Jesus Christ which we call the church. Of course, the use of the word *sacrament* in this context worries some people. "Oh," they warn, "we should be careful of talking about the church as a sacrament because Christ instituted only two sacraments—the Lord's Supper and baptism." I appreciate the force of this argument and have every sympathy for the desire to protect what is important. I wish to argue, however, that this is quite compatible with the notion of the church as a sacrament.

First, we need to define what we mean by the word *sacrament*.[7] The word comes from the Latin word *sacramentum,* which means a "pledge." It was used in the ancient world of the oath of a Roman soldier who declared his allegiance to Caesar. However, its meaning in the church acquired a far richer significance because the word was used to translate the Greek word *mysterion* ("mystery"). Thus a sacrament came to be regarded as something more than what it seemed to be; it pointed beyond itself to a deeper level of reality. In time a sacrament was defined as "an outward and visible sign of an inward and spiritual grace." So then, a sacrament, in the broadest sense of the word, is a sign of some deeper reality, and in a real, although intangible sense, it conveys something special.

A wedding ring can be sacramental. It symbolizes the commitment of two people to one another. That romantic moment when the transaction is sealed in a church with the giving of a ring is a sacred moment. The ring itself will forever remain as a seal of that event. Whether it is a cheap piece of tin or a priceless jewel is beside the point—the meaning and occasion count. If the girl loses the ring, the well-intentioned remark "Oh never mind, I will buy you a replacement tomorrow" will not help. There are other moments in life which we might call sacramental—vows or promises between friends, the giving of one's life to Jesus Christ, that moment in prayer when you have got up convinced that in God's good time that prayer *will* be answered.

But in an orthodox Christian sense a sacrament is more than a sign. It is also effective. Again, to use an ordinary illustration, when a child is adopted the legal documents are not only a *sign* to the parents that Kirsti is their child, they are an *effective* symbol which declares a new status.[8] Ink and paper they may be, and only worth a few dollars, but for parents and child the documents state something that is timeless and priceless. The documents will stand as a perpetual reminder of promises which have an abiding value.

We shall see the relevance of this to Holy Communion and baptism later, but for the moment I want to point out the Protestant churches' curious silence about the sacramental reality of the church—in spite of the fact that we believe in it! It may well be that, because the concept of the church was so crucial for the Roman Catholic Church's understanding of itself, Protestant churches in reaction have ignored it, despite the fact that the idea of the visible body has always been of importance for most Protestant bodies. It would, indeed, be rare to find a Christian who did not believe in the church. People rightly become Christians in or through the church. "Robinson Crusoe" Christianity is not the norm. Only in exceptional circumstances— persecution, for example—are Christians given strength to stand alone. Some of the mutineers of H.M.S. Bounty, we might recall, discovered Jesus Christ through reading the Bible on their desert island, but that experience is far from normal. And, in any case, what took place created a Christian community!

In a real sense then, the gospel of Jesus Christ and the church of Jesus Christ are inseparably connected. Of course, we do not and we should not preach the church. It is belief in Jesus Christ as Lord that makes a person a Christian. Yet whatever denomination we belong to, we know that without the church we cannot stand as Christians, grow as Christians, or enjoy the faith as Christians. When we have the great joy of helping another human being to find a living faith in Jesus Christ, we do not say, "Now go away and try to live the Christian life." Instead we say, "It is important for you to join a Christian fellowship where you can discover more of the Christian faith and know the support and encouragement of God's family." No doubt we would encourage our friend to join a discipleship course and, if not baptized, to express his newfound faith in the sacramental act of baptism.

We must emphasize again, that by describing the church as sacramental we are not implying that everyone has to adopt Catholic customs concerning the sacraments. Of course not. We are simply saying that there is a common realization that God takes the visible body of the church seriously and manifests his grace in it. It is his body, and he gives life to it.

Two factors of importance flow from this understanding of the visible body. First, the church is a sacramental sign of God's work on earth. In spite of our weakness, disunity and deficiencies, the church bears witness to God who cares enough about us to die for us. In spite of our sin we believe that God does not reject us but that his grace works within us, his body. That grace is effective too. It comes to us through the preaching of God's Word, through such sacraments as baptism and the Lord's Supper, through the ministry of encouragement as we meet in fellowship, and in many other different ways as the Holy Spirit works among us.

Turning to the links between the Catholic and Protestant churches, it is understandable that Roman Catholics should be proud of their church, which has retained its identity and its unity over the years. Its historical manifestation is impressive and so is its spiritual and moral vitality. But Protestants too can be proud of their own church and the courageous stand for truth that their church fathers have taken. Division is, of course, a sad blot on the church's history, but Christians separated in the past because they cared passionately for the truth and they wished that truth to be preserved within the fellowship of Christ's family.

The church then, in short, is not an optional extra. To be "in Christ," says the New Testament, is to be "in the church." To be a Christian at all is to belong to other Christian believers. That is why it is intolerable when Christians of one denomination write off other believers. At one time the Catholic Church rejected all other Christians, claiming itself alone to be the one true church. At a stroke it not only dechurched millions of other Christians, but it also implied that they were not true believers at all. Although this attitude is still encountered, it is rare today.

Again a major breakthrough from the Catholic side can be seen in the Second Vatican Council, which expressed two important elements in its understanding of the church. First, it acknowledged the reality of other Christian communities besides its own. While it continued to assert that the church of Christ *subsists* in the Roman Catholic Church, it did not lay claim to being the *only* true Christian body.[9] Second, the ecclesiology of the Council made a distinction between the church and its historical manifestations. In other words, this church, at once local and universal, embraces more than the Catholic Church. It is the whole body of Christ: Catholics, Orthodox, Anglicans, Methodists and so on. Although Vatican II did not recognize all churches as equal, the progress of Catholic thought on this issue is most exciting.[10] The pre-Vatican II concept that the Roman Catholic Church is the one true church was set aside in favor of a more mystical and spiritual understanding of the church. As a result, since the Council the Catholic Church in many parts of the world has gone out of its way to affirm the value of other traditions.

The second factor which flows from taking the visible body of the church on earth seriously is the necessity of our wrestling with the tension between the church's holiness and sinfulness. It may be a hard thing to hear, but we shall not progress far in our quest for unity until there is greater honesty about the church's sinfulness as well as its holiness. Without a general recognition of the church as erring and failing, we are unlikely to arrive at the truth we share. Catholic emphasis on the *inerrancy* of the church makes it nearly impossible for the Catholic Church to even come close to admitting error in matters of dogma.

From a Protestant viewpoint it seems only too clear that the church has and does err. Christian history is marked by failure, error, mistakes of all kinds. Some popes have not lived up to their high office and have misled the faithful. To say this is only to recognize the humanity of leadership. No one is perfect. Now, Catholics fully recognize the sinfulness of the church in the failings, faithlessness and errors of its members. Indeed, the Catholic Church has a long history of reform movements which have arisen in order to bring the church back to doctrinal and behavioral purity. In his own day St. Ignatius of Loyola argued that his critical attitude to the official church was due to his love for the church as the bride of Christ. Such an attitude, he said, was essentially devout if it led to the church rediscovering its vocation in winning souls.[11]

Catholic Christians must excuse the temerity of their Protestant brethren who are puzzled about how the sinfulness of the church could fail to affect doctrinal purity. If the Vatican II *Decree on Ecumenism* acknowledges that both sides were to blame for the divisions of the church, does this not *inevitably* entail doctrinal misunderstanding and error? If the Catholic Church insists that it has been preserved by God's grace from error in its teaching, how can true dialog take place? What doctrinal room, indeed, is there in which to maneuver?

Perhaps Catholics and Protestants together need to rediscover the New Testament idea of the holiness of the church. As with individuals, the church as a body is only holy "in Christ." It has no intrinsic holiness of its own. Recognizing that our holiness is in Christ clothes the church, not only with Christ's righteousness, but also with hope, because it cannot be and will not be God's intention to desert his church, however disobedient it becomes. Hope reassures the people of God that through God's Spirit it will maintain its witness and will be preserved from gross error. This is a completely different view from maintaining that the church is preserved from all error. To assert the latter is to confuse the future reality with present hope, and it may lead to triumphalism and complacency.

Faith

Faith is another area where Catholics and Protestants share a common base, and yet where long-standing differences have obscured certain agreements.

In Catholic parlance *faith* or *the faith* commonly means the faith of the church. It represents the doctrinal standpoint of the church, expressed in the creeds and in definitive theological dogmas and utterances. Faith is, therefore, seen as a firm assent of the mind to what the church authoritatively teaches in the name of God. It tends to be thought of as intellectual submission and obedience. The classic expression of this is found in St. Augustine's epigrammatic statement, "I should not believe the gospel unless the authority of the Catholic Church moved me to do so."[12]

Protestant scholars have criticized this intellectualist notion of faith. They point out that it makes God a revealer of sacred doctrine instead of Redeemer, and it puts the church in the role of dispenser of truth. In addition, they point out, this interpretation slights the personal element in the biblical understanding of faith. Some go even further in their criticism. The Catholic understanding of faith, they argue, focuses a person's attention so strongly on what should be believed and obeyed with the mind that the moral and political implications of faith are ignored.

For Protestants *faith* has generally meant personal belief and trust. This is sometimes called the *fiducial* approach. It emphasizes the personal relationship of the believer with God. Catholic objections to this have been twofold. First, to say that I am saved by my faith in Christ seems to imply that it is *my* faith which saves. It smacks of subjectivism, bypassing the church or even the objective facts of the Christian message. Second, Catholics warn, such an emphasis may lead to an unbiblical pietism which undermines social responsibility and concern for the kingdom of God.

Over the last ten years or so I have noticed in Great Britain a remarkable coming together in our understanding of faith in Christ. We have begun to see that faith has two levels: corporate faith *(fides)* and personal trust *(fiducia)*. Both are essential.

The faith of the church is necessary for Christian belief. I cannot go my own way; I am called to identify with the deposit of faith. For nearly two thousand years the Christian church has hammered out its belief structure, and we need to submit to it to call ourselves Christians. I cannot say "I believe in Christ—a tremendous guy—but of course I don't believe he was the Son of God." That might make me a Christian camp-follower, but not a Christian. The Christian church is clear that we don't come on our own terms; we come on God's.

And the second dimension of faith is crucial too. It would be odd to say "I'm afraid I have no personal faith in Jesus Christ as God's Son. But if the church requires me to assent to it, I will do so. I'll let the church believe for me." This idea was not uncommon a few decades ago among Catholic well-wishers who liked the church but were agnostic about their beliefs. The Christian answer is simple. Your personal assent is required; no equivocation is allowable.

But what is the character of faith if it is personal and corporate? Essentially, it is belief in Christ as Savior. He alone has dealt decisively with the problem of sin, death and alienation. I have discovered two ways in which Catholics and Protestants are saying similar things about this faith in Christ.

First, both traditions acknowledge that he is the *only* way. Both traditions make absolute claims for Christ. This is not to say that God cannot work through other religions. But it is to claim that in a final and decisive way God has spoken through Jesus and continues to speak. It has been a great joy to me to share platforms and to be on committees with Roman Catholic theologians who are devoted to Christ and his revelation. We have shared a common base which separates us from those who have wanted to blur the distinctiveness of Jesus of Nazareth.

Second, I find today a growing emphasis that *trust* in Jesus Christ is the only secure way of salvation. It used to be said, "Scratch a Roman Catholic and you'll find an old-fashioned Pelagian underneath." Pelagius, we may recall, was a fifth-century British monk who took issue with the famous theologian Augustine. Augustine had argued that man cannot save himself; he is saved only by God's grace. Pelagius asserted to the contrary that we can initiate salvation by our own good works. Now, no one disputes the importance of good deeds. Show us a person who claims to be a Christian and yet lives a dubious life, and we will have grounds to believe that that person is a hypocrite. But a good life is a fragile foundation for faith because it is *my* goodness. Augustine argued instead that the cross is the only sufficient basis for salvation and that good deeds are our response to God's free gift of life. A good life is the *fruit*, not the *root*, of the Christian life. A Catholic monk once shared with me his understanding of his own sacrificial life. It flowed, he said, from an expression of gratitude to Jesus Christ who loved him and gave himself for him.

Now this element of praise is crucially important because it emphasizes that something has been done, something given, something achieved. You don't launch into praise and thanksgiving unless something noteworthy has happened. Ask any final-year student! The New Testament throbs with joy, thanksgiving and praise because of what Christ has achieved. Indeed, the only fitting sacrifice we can offer is that of praise and thanksgiving. This makes God's deeds primary and ours a response. The charismatic renewal movement has emphasized this quality of thanksgiving and in so doing has drawn attention to the full and complete benefits won for us on the cross.

I have been astonished by the common agreement reached by charismatics of all kinds—Catholic and Protestant—that it is through simple, believing trust in Jesus that our sins are dealt with and the Spirit is given. This New Testament faith is often obscured by our traditions. It may be brushed aside by a Catholic tendency to stress our need to cooperate with divine grace. Or it may be overlaid by the Protestant work ethic, which makes salvation seem a heavy and difficult affair. A friend of mine once said, "Christ did not call men to an idle and frivolous life. He did not say, 'Come, lie on my cushion!' He said, 'Come, take up your cross and follow me.' But he also said, 'My yoke is easy and my burden is light.' Thank God that he has also given us his Holy Spirit to make the Christian road a delightful thing."

If there is a converging understanding of faith as both personal trust and assent to a body of doctrine, there is a third understanding of the character of faith which is receiving great support today from both Catholic and Protestant leaders.[13] This is an understanding of faith as commitment to God's action in the world. Faith is more than just belief or simple trust; it is expressed in action. This is biblical. The letter of James unites belief and action to draw out the true meaning of faith—"faith without works is dead." So true faith can never be a matter of unrelated words; it must be incarnated in action or in praxis, as some theologians prefer to term it.

This understanding of faith has both Catholic and Protestant adherents, especially among those who sympathize with the liberation theology movement. Those who hold this theology believe that faith is not passive but an active commitment to the gospel of Christ united with a hearty desire to establish the values of the kingdom in society.

Thus Catholics and Protestants alike are discovering more and more the New Testament dimension of living in the faith of Christ. We may rightly hope that, as we seek to explore the challenge of living closely with Jesus Christ, Lord of all, we will find that faith in him eclipses the sad bitterness and misunderstanding of the past.

The Holy Communion

One of the central issues of the Reformation was the status of the Mass or Holy Communion service. Although both sides agreed that Jesus died for our sins, there was sharp controversy over how that salvation was made available. Roman Catholics held that in the Mass Christ continued to make available his life for believers as he was re-presented before the Father. The Mass was seen as an "unbloody" sacrifice that dealt with sin as Christ came again to his people to give them his life.

Catholic theologians argued further that the words of institution—"This is my body; this is my blood"—supported the doctrine of transubstantiation. This doctrine holds that the substance of the bread and wine of Holy Communion are transformed into the substance of Christ's body and blood. Only the appearance of the bread and wine remain. Transubstantiation is one philosophical means of explaining the real presence of Christ in the sacrament of Holy Communion.

Protestant thinking recoiled sharply from the Catholic view on both counts. First, the Reformers took issue with the notion that the Mass is a sacrifice, other than a sacrifice of praise and thanksgiving. Catholic teaching, later defined in the Council of Trent, held that there is a continuity between the Last Supper of Jesus and the eucharistic offering of the church. At the Last Supper Christ offered his body and blood under the species of bread and wine, and he commanded the apostles and their successors to present the same offering. Hence the Mass is a *real* sacrifice and the human priest is the representative of Christ who acts in his place. Similarly the victim is the same as it was on Calvary, only here it is offered in an unbloody manner. The eucharistic sacrifice is then the effective means by which our daily sins are forgiven.

The Reformers argued that this understanding deviated from biblical Christianity. I do not intend to go into this aspect in any depth except to mention two arguments used by the Reformers. They argued first that the Catholic doctrine of the Mass diminished the importance of Christ's death. Because Calvary was a once-for-all event that dealt decisively with sin, there is no longer any need to re-present a sin offering or to plead Christ's merits. Christ's death is the atonement which brings us freedom and life. The proper response at Holy Communion is therefore thankful hearts. Then, they contended, Catholic theology made the priest another Christ and, by implication, another mediator. This was, they considered, a dangerous error, which not only united the priest's functions with Christ's, but also separated the priest from the laity because the priest drew his ministry not from the church but from his sacerdotal ministry in Christ.

The other count on which Protestants recoiled from Catholic views was the identification of Jesus with the bread of Communion. This is not to say, however, that they were united in their interpretation of the words "This is my body." Martin Luther had a very high doctrine of the Lord's Supper and took the words literally, although he rejected the notion of a change of substance in the bread. Other Reformers were more radical. Some understood the words "This is my body" metaphorically, arguing these words were to be understood similarly to Jesus' words "I am the door"; others held that Jesus was present in the celebration but by faith only. Indeed, the word *hocus-pocus,* meaning nonsense or tomfoolery, has long been thought to have originated in the phrase *hoc est corpus meum* ("this is my body") and thus may well represent a lingering taint of the bitterness which marked the controversy of the sixteenth century.

Strangely enough, few have remarked on the fact that behind the problem are areas of agreement. First, the two sides agreed on the importance of Holy Communion. It was instituted by Christ and was his last word and testament. He wanted this rite to continue.

Second, we have always agreed on the spiritual value of the service. Paul speaks against those in the Corinthian church who did not discern the Lord's body and clearly saw the Lord's Supper as a sacred rite, a means of having a meal with one another and with the risen Lord. "For as often as you eat this bread and drink the cup, you proclaim the Lord's death until he comes" (1 Cor 11:26). In that statement Paul unites the past, present and future. Holy Communion links the two comings of Christ. No doubt, Paul believed that the risen Christ was the host at the fellowship meal.

Third, we agree that Jesus intended something with the bread and wine. He identified himself with the bread and the wine. It is his body which is broken and his blood which is poured out for many. Whether we take a physicalist notion that this means literally Christ's body, or a metaphorical idea, there is general agreement among Christians that the elements are the locus for Christ's presence in some form.

Now in what ways have Catholics and Protestants moved closer together in their understanding of the real presence? First, as Peter Toon makes clear from a study of the confessional statements of the Reformers, although they rejected the medieval doctrine of transubstantiation, they commonly and heartily agreed that there is *true* fellowship with the Lord Jesus and a *true* participation in him in Holy Communion.[14] The Lord's Supper is a real spiritual communion with Christ. The intent of the Reformers was not to suggest a "real absence" but to emphasize Christ's spiritual presence while downplaying the physical aspects which they felt had been abused. Thus both sides held in common that in this sacred act Christ is present in a special way.

Second, dialog between Christians these days tends to be less polemical than in former times, and this relaxing of tension has led to fresh understandings of the notion of the presence of Christ. Let us examine this term a little more closely. When we talk of someone being present, we can mean three different things at least. The first meaning is that of *temporal presence*, so we say, "Yesterday my back was troubling me. I had a lot of pain." That is, we felt the presence of pain yesterday. That kind of presence is opposed to the past and the future.

There is, secondly, *spatial presence*. The mother who sees her son going to university will say, "I'll miss him." That is, she'll miss his spatial presence. That kind of presence is opposed to distance.

There is a third kind of presence which philosophers call *personal presence*. The son who is going off to university might respond to his mother, "Don't worry, Mother, I'll write and phone you twice a week. You are always in my thoughts." This kind of presence is able to transcend both space and time.[15]

Now when we talk about God being present we have to remember the inadequacy of our space-time categories to explain fully what we mean and want to say. We know that when Jesus lived in Nazareth he was localized in such a way that it limited him from being, say, in Jerusalem at the same time. But now that he has ascended we believe that as Lord he is present with his people whether we live in New York or Paris. The concept of personal presence, therefore, may help us understand that Christ is really present with us in Communion while not explaining the ultimate mystery of how he makes the elements of bread and wine the means of his presence.

Third, a great deal of questioning of the doctrine of transubstantiation has taken place during recent years.[16] A substantial number of Catholics believe that the idea of transubstantiation is philosophically unacceptable today. The reason is simple. Philosophically the concept depends on the notion that reality is composed of external "accidents" (shape, weight, color) and internal substances which are the true reality. Transubstantiation, as originally defined, meant that the substance of Christ entered into the accidents of the wafer, so that the accidents remained while the substance of the wafer was replaced by Christ himself. Now if this doctrine no longer finds philosophical support, how are we to understand the idea of a real presence?

Because of the problems inherent in the medieval view of transubstantiation, a number of Dutch Catholic theologians, notably Edward Schillebeeckx, have attempted to explain the real presence without employing the term.[17] They draw attention to the *sign* that is at the center of the Eucharist. This sign unites the past with the present and the believer with his Lord. As the ordinary elements of bread and wine are taken, they are impregnated with meaning as Christ's words are recalled and as his death is remembered. They become for us, therefore, signs which bear a new meaning: signs of the glorious reality of the life of Christ. This view is called *transignification*. The same Catholic theologians also speak of a new purpose *(transfinalization)* which the sign acquires as a eucharistic symbol.

It must be acknowledged that this desire to find new ways of expressing the reality of Christ in the elements of Holy Communion has not won acceptance among all Catholics. Indeed, in 1965 Pope Paul VI's encyclical *Mysterium fidei* reasserted the traditional doctrine of transubstantiation, emphasizing the ontic reality of Christ in the sacrament.

It is clear, however, that since the Second Vatican Council Catholic scholars and leaders have been much more open to honest investigation of their concept of the real presence, and new understandings have emerged from recent Catholic statements. The Second Vatican Council insisted that the presence of Christ is not confined to the consecrated elements; Christ is present in the community and he is also present in the Word proclaimed. Furthermore, dialog between Catholics and Protestants has revealed agreement about the reality of meeting Jesus Christ under the signs of bread and wine.[18]

The Lutheran-Catholic Consultation as well as the Anglican-Roman Catholic International Commission have produced fundamental agreement on the "that" of the real presence, even if they have not agreed on the "how." The Anglican-Roman Catholic discussion on the Eucharist is sensitively aware that for many people, particularly Protestants, transubstantiation is not the best way to explain the meaning of Christ's presence with us sacramentally. The term *transubstantiation* is consequently relegated to a footnote with the explanation that it is a way of understanding the reality present in this feast of the church.

Although many problems remain, especially with the idea that the Mass is a sacrifice offered to God, signs of convergence are beginning to appear. In Roman Catholic circles Holy Communion is often given in both kinds to the laity; there is less talk of transubstantiation, though no loss of a sense of the personal presence of Christ; there is a greater awareness of the real presence of Christ through means other than the consecrated elements; there is a deeper appreciation of the spiritual character of the eucharistic meal. Further progress will not likely be made until both Catholics and Protestants are less bound and restricted by Medieval and Reformation formularies, and more firmly anchored in New Testament teaching and early church practice. We must allow the original sources to stimulate and refresh our understanding, and, more important, our study of the documents should be done, not apart, but together, so that creative and sympathetic dialog may end in shared perspectives.

In this chapter we have looked at five key areas of doctrine and have tried to show how much common ground exists between Protestants and Catholics. While some observers may prefer to begin with points of difference, I fear that in doing so we end up denying to one another the charity the gospel commands us to give. Many of us are fond of singing "We are one in the spirit; we are one in the Lord." The chorus of that song ends, "And they'll know we are Christians by our love, by our love: yes, they'll know we are Christians by our love." That love is at the heart of the Christian profession, and if the most orthodox Protestant or Catholic has not the charity which longs to draw others in, we may rightly question that person's faith. The zealot looks for the points that divide; the lover seizes on the things held in common.

Thomas Aquinas, one of the greatest Catholic theologians, wrote, *"Ubi amor, ibi oculus"* ("Where there is love there is vision")—that is, knowing and loving are inseparably linked. D. L. Moody, the great American evangelist from a completely different tradition, once remarked, "If you go through the world with love in your heart, you will make the world love you, and love is the badge that Christ gave his disciples." Both great men emphasized the centrality of love—the first in theology, the second in life. Without question, had Christians in the past shown greater love to one another, the course of history would have been different. And, very possibly, if we today display greater charity and magnanimity to other Christians and other traditions, we too may be able to influence the course of events and create a new environment in which we can grow together. I argue this way not to suggest that truth is not important, nor yet to suggest that all the problems that remain will be solved through a loving attitude alone, but I am certain that without love for one another we will never resolve our differences.

In the next two chapters we shall consider the respective strengths of the Catholic and Protestant traditions in the hope that we might arrive at a better understanding of one another.

Chapter 5
THE
RESERVOIR
OF ROME

*I*n March 1982, when the Archbishop of Canterbury arrived in Liverpool to give a lunch-time address, he had a totally unexpected and alarming welcome. About a hundred protesters, described by the national press as an "angry, banner-waving mob," jeered the archbishop because of his pronounced views on the issue of unity. His address was constantly interrupted by cries of "Judas," "Hang him," "traitor" and so on. The verbal attacks occurred even when he was praying. Such an uproar, especially against the primate of the Anglican Church, was very surprising even in Liverpool, which has had a long history of sectarian bitterness.

Whatever we may think about such demonstrations, the attitude of these protesters was uncompromisingly clear: Rome is unreformed and the true Christian must have no link with her. She is the great "harlot" of Revelation 13.

What I want to explore in this chapter is diametrically opposed to that spirit. I wish to ask, "What may we learn from the Catholic tradition? What is distinctive about Catholicism? In what ways does it challenge other Christian churches?" While I certainly intend to present Protestant objections to Catholic claims, it is important that we should try to understand thoughtfully its contribution to worldwide Christianity.[1]

A Historical Church

What do we think of when we think about the church? Is it the building on the corner, the church with associations which go back into our family's history and memory, or perhaps the fellowship we are in at the moment? It is not unknown for evangelical Christians to worship in an evangelical Baptist church one year and then move on to an evangelical Episcopal or Free church the next year, and so on if their work or other factors take them away. Protestants in the main have suffered from having a weak doctrine of the church. They have viewed the church as a fellowship of like-minded people or a body "which agrees with me."

The Catholic view of the church takes the historical dimension of the body very seriously. Its claim is that it alone has an unbroken succession which can be traced back to the infant church. The Pope's emphasis on his historical link with the apostle Peter, the claim that the teachings of present-day Catholicism conform to the teachings of the early church—all this and more are believed to be marks of an ancient church rooted in New Testament Christianity. Indeed, it is possible to argue that Catholicism's distinctive ecclesiological feature is the importance assigned to the Petrine ministry of the Bishop of Rome.

This claim is usually contested in two ways. First, the Orthodox Church of the East denies Rome's exclusive claim, arguing that the Orthodox Church is also a historical church anchored in the ancient church. The churches of Jerusalem, Antioch and Alexandria are in no way inferior to Rome. Indeed, Orthodox theologians claim, it was Rome's imperialistic attitude in the eleventh century which led to the split between Western and Eastern churches. This anchorage in the bedrock of the primitive church is also shared by the churches of the East, they assert. This counterclaim certainly has its force, but even the most die-hard Orthodox Christian will admit that from the fourth century the Bishop of Rome was given a place of honor and usually seen as the focal point of unity.

Second, from the Protestant side, the argument from history is usually treated with respect tinged with skepticism. Historical continuity, it is said, is beside the point if the church bears little resemblance to the church of the New Testament. Development can end in *re*gression as well as *pro*gression. This is certainly so and reminds us that the argument from antiquity is not cogent if the New Testament does not support it clearly.[2]

Nevertheless the Catholic Church has a strong historical identity based on its claim of unity with the past; one has only to go to Rome, the Eternal City, and walk the Via Appia, visiting the catacombs and such ancient churches as San Clemente, St. John Lateran and many more to be reminded of this fact. Cardinal John Newman, in his famous book *An Essay on the Development of Christian Doctrine,* claimed that "no one can deny that the body of doctrine which at the time goes by the name of Catholic is at once the historical and the logical continuation of the body of doctrine so called in the eighteenth, in the seventeenth, in the sixteenth, and so back in every preceding century successively till we come to the fifth. Whether it be a corrupt development, or a legitimate, conducted on sound logic or fallacious, the present so-called Catholic religion is the successor, the representative and the heir of the religion of the so-called Catholic Church of primitive times."[3]

From this historical consciousness arises the belief that the church is the mother of the faithful. What this means is that Catholics are taught to regard their church as handing on the truth which can be trusted and must be obeyed. The faith of Catholics is therefore the faith of the church, and they believe because the church believes. The doctrine of the church is not *external* to the gospel; it is *part* of the gospel.

Walther von Loewenich draws attention to the significance of the church for the Catholic faith. "The Church," he says, citing Konrad Algermissen, "is the central idea of Catholicism. The doctrine of the Church is the issue which divides the denominations today. Catholic faith is in the last resort faith in the Church."[4] It may well be the case that Catholic Christians brought up in the more tolerant spirit of Vatican II will see this as a sweeping generalization, but there is a great deal of truth in the statement. We have already seen in the case of a number of Catholic teachings—notably concerning the authority of the Scriptures and the Marian dogmas—that at the heart of both is the church's self-consciousness as guardian of the truth. But what there can be little doubt about is that the Catholic Church has traditionally viewed itself as a divine institution, founded by Christ, and on Christ's promise to Peter; and because Peter was given jurisdiction over his brethren, the church is kept infallibly free from doctrinal error. The visible, hierarchical church is consequently identified with the body of Christ, confident that it incarnates the presence of Christ in the world.

This view of the church was at the heart of Reformation issues, although, curiously, it did not hold great prominence. Many of Luther's Catholic opponents agreed with him that the church needed reform, but they parted company from him when it seemed he was criticizing the fundamental nature of the church. They believed that they could put the house in order by dealing with certain abuses like indulgences and by making such doctrinal reforms as were necessary. Luther's attack, however, on the papacy, priesthood, Eucharist and ministry required a radical restructuring of the church, which many felt attacked its very nature.

Today, with the benefit of hindsight, we may endorse the valid points that both sides were making in support of their case. Many Catholics today, for example, agree that the Reformers' great stress on Jesus and the nature of salvation was a proper reminder of the character of New Testament Christianity. Yet these great truths, loosened from a secure doctrine of the church, in time led to serious weakness in the Protestant faith. As subjective notions of the church prevailed, Protestants lost sense of historical continuity. In modern terms we could say that an existential approach replaced the historical. Thus the character of preaching, or defining what the church stands for, became the touchstone of what is or is not genuine Christianity.

This led to the inevitable fragmentation of the church.

Even today, the genius of Protestantism consists in its ability to assemble enthusiastic, godly groups of people bound together in a deep love for Jesus, with a conviction that they have a special calling to establish a new fellowship. The tragedy of Protestantism is the ease with which it drifts from its roots in history, society and culture. But we cannot deny or ignore the past. Our faith is handed down to us from the past, and to refuse to learn the lessons of history usually results, ironically, in being conditioned by contemporary history and thus ending up less adaptable to the present. Protestants, therefore, cannot fail to gain something from the Catholic doctrine of the church. At the very least, we might develop a greater respect and love for the church which has nurtured us and, perhaps, a deeper loyalty to its teachings. In so doing, we may gain a better understanding of our place within it. There can be little hesitation that the unity of Catholicism is in itself an attractive thing to many people.

If the weakness of Protestants has been to underestimate the historical reality we call the church, the weakness of Catholics has been a failure to appreciate that the church stands under the gospel of Jesus and is always called to be renewed. The Second Vatican Council, however, altered the assumption that the church never changes. Following the call for *aggiornamento* ("renewal"), Catholic ecclesiology has carried forward the insights of the church as a pilgrim people.

In addition to recognizing other churches and Christians as belonging to the body of Christ, Catholics have begun to emphasize the subordination of the church to the kingdom, to see the need for ongoing institutional reform, and to desire the unity of the entire church.

True historical continuity with the past, therefore, involves the critical task of evaluating church life in the light of the apostolic commission. Appeals to past authorities, whether Catholic or Protestant, are not enough. Much as we all love the security of authority figures and find it deeply comforting to say "Einstein said . . . Darwin wrote . . . Billy Graham says . . . the Pope teaches . . .

the magisterium writes . . . my minister preaches . . . "—none of these is above the authority of Christ as revealed in Scripture.

A Church in Society

We have just touched on the Protestant tendency to drift into ghetto forms of Christianity. This is a rather sweeping generalization, but most of us will recognize some truth in it. It is all too tempting for Christians to meet in cozy fellowships away from the real problems of the world. When I began my ministry in a tough part of North London, there was in one part of our parish a closed Independent Fellowship which came together every Sunday morning. Each Sunday they drove in from different parts of the city. They took the chains off the door and welcomed all in fellowship with them to worship. I was clearly not in fellowship with them, because when I tried one Sunday to join them they refused to admit me. What was significant and sad was that after their time of worship together they locked and chained up their building and disappeared from the district.

Of course, this is not typical of all Protestants. But it does indicate the extremes to which some Christians go to affirm their brand of faith, which as a result appears to be otherworldly and isolated from the problems of secular society. Evangelical Christians in Britain and the United States are now much more actively involved in political and social action than they have been in the past, but we still need to learn more about incarnating the values of Christ in a dark and fallen world.

Here, again, Protestants can learn a great deal from a second characteristic of Catholicism—that is, the incarnational involvement of the church in the world. Our model for such incarnation is Jesus. Just as he was involved in his society and lived among men and women, witnessing to the presence of the kingdom of God, so the church must become imbedded in the real world and not isolated from it. In theory, if not always in practice, this has been the ideal of all Christian bodies. But it has consistently been a strong element in the Catholic doctrine of the church during the past century. In education, social care, medical care, political action, to name but a few areas, Catholic influence has been considerable. Not only in Poland, where the church exercises a mediatorial position between a Communist regime and the trade-union movement, but in many developing countries as well, the Catholic Church has not shrunk from defending human rights and Christian ideals, even in the face of bitter oppression.

Monsignor Oscar Romero, Archbishop of San Salvador, was an inspiring example of such courage. A small man, no more than five feet tall, he made up for his lack of height by a directness of style. Against an unjust regime in El Salvador, which denied the poor even the most basic of human rights, he appealed for a compassionate social policy which would release the oppressed from economic slavery. The irony was that when Romero was appointed archbishop in 1977 he was regarded as a soft touch, a timid prelate who would pose no problems. But he was drawn more and more into the center of the conflict.

He began with the gospel. He encouraged clergy and parishes to work out from the message of Jesus what the Christian estimate of humanity is. He joined many progressive priests in attacking the accepted notion that God makes some people rich and the majority poor. He encouraged the search for a Christian understanding of values, to discover what freedom means to a poor man, what human dignity is to those bereft of education and culture. He was bold to ask if passivity is indeed always a Christian virtue. Is protest necessarily wrong? If it is not wrong to defend oneself against evil, is it wrong to resist those who deprive you of those basic human rights which are yours as much as theirs? The policy was, according to one priest, to "put feet on the gospel."

Three years later Romero died in a bloody, spectacular fashion. Just before Easter 1980 he celebrated Mass in a hospital near his cathedral. As he raised the chalice high, a shot rang out and Romero collapsed, his own blood mingling with the spilt wine from the chalice which lay nearby.

What Romero experienced so violently many Catholic priests, nuns and lay folk have encountered less dramatically in other ways. A Catholic friend told me about a friend of his who was a priest in another South American country. His congregation included a number of trade-union officials who were well known for their outspoken views against the Fascist government. Because the priest was a friend of these men, he too was regarded as a marked man. Suddenly one day these trade-union officials were taken away without trial. Eventually, reports reached the church that the men were being tortured severely. The following day during the Mass the priest read the set reading from Amos, which spoke of God's anger against all who oppose justice. The priest was arrested after the service and charged with libelous use of the Bible. He was released only when he pointed out that the reading was that appointed for the day. It was in fact Scripture which condemned them, and it spoke clearly against the oppression.

Of course, Rome's incarnational approach can be romanticized. An incarnational approach does not characterize the whole of the Catholic Church, nor has it always been at the forefront of the church's concerns. Catholicism has occasionally withdrawn into the security of its own life and piety. Nevertheless, other churches have much to learn from its witness in many areas of social concern over the last hundred years.[5] As Richard McBrien explains, Catholic social doctrine only developed toward the end of the last century.[6] As it developed it became clearly discernible as a body of official teachings on the social order in its economic and political dimensions. The starting point was Leo XIII's encyclical *Rerum Novarum* ("On the Condition of the Workingman") in 1891. According to Walther von Loewenich, *Rerum Novarum* has become the Magna Charta of Christian social ethics. Based on Christian principles, the encyclical appeals for a just society in which workers will receive their proper share of the distribution of wealth. Although from our vantage point it is a pity that socialism is lumped with Communism and dismissed, a great deal of the encyclical is a powerful statement of Christian social theology. In the context of its own day it was an inspiring, imaginative and prophetic statement of Christian concern for industrial society. Thus *Rerum Novarum* articulated in a systematic manner a theology of social justice. Later popes built on this solid foundation to confront the growth of secularism and materialism and the threat of a world-dominating Communism with a moral framework for the political and economic questions which face the human family.

The Second Vatican Council took Catholic social theory to a wholly different stage when it forged a link between the social ministry of the church and its nature and mission. The *Pastoral Constitution on the Church in the Modern World* stressed such elements as the dignity of the human person created in the image of God, the dignity of the moral conscience, the fundamental equality of human beings, the social nature of human existence and the freedom of the individual. This constitution, together with the document *Justice in the World*, called for action on behalf of justice, urging Christians to strive for the transformation of the world.

There can be little doubt that this call for Catholics to become involved in the struggle for justice encouraged South American theologians and church leaders such as Gustavo Gutierrez to articulate a distinctively Latin American theological perspective, which has become known as liberation theology.

All this is not to say that Protestants have ignored the needs of society. We have only to point to evangelicals like Wilberforce, who led the antislavery campaign, to Methodists who shaped the British Trade Union Movement, to Lord Shaftesbury and the creation of the Factory Laws which alleviated many of the problems surrounding child labor, and to William Temple and the formation of Christian socialism, to name but a few of the Protestants who have shared the desire to bring Christian insight to bear on society. But by and large such activity has reflected inspiring individual initiative rather than the collective effort of Protestant Christians standing boldly for Christian moral principles.

Nevertheless, both Catholic and Protestant Christians agree that the Christian faith must engage the needs of society, that the gospel bears political significance. If Christ came to break the power of evil—to care for the poor, liberate those in bondage, educate the unlearned—his people cannot stand aloof from human pain and misery. We have a duty to represent the oppressed and deprived and to care about moral issues and values.

In this common concern for the human family is a very real "meeting of the waters" that holds exciting possibilities for our quest for unity. Protestants cannot but admire the Catholic stand for the dignity of every human being as exemplified in documents like *Familiaris Consortio* (1981)—a splendid presentation of family life and the mutual care and love we should give one another. On the practical level, in many prolife campaigns against liberal abortion laws, Catholics and Protestants are actively working together for the welfare of unborn children.

Catholic readers, however, must forgive me if I end this section on a more critical note. If I have charged Protestants with overemphasizing the spiritual side of the gospel and neglecting the social dimension, I feel constrained to point out a common criticism of the Catholic social ethic; namely, Rome's concern for human rights is hindered by its attitude to contraception. Pope Paul VI's encyclical *Humanae Vitae* (1968) had many excellent things to say about marriage and human love, but the Pope's judgment on contraception has overshadowed all else. All that most people know about the document is that it condemns contraception, which is declared to be intrinsically wrong and on the same level as abortion and sterilization.[7]

Contraception is, of course, a serious moral issue. It is well known that, while in more developed nations contraceptive family planning is widely practiced by Catholic Christians, in many poorer countries Rome's rigid approach has hindered the rise of the poor from their bondage. John Whale, for example, criticized Pope John Paul II's strong stand against artificial birth control during his visits to Latin American countries, noting that "if the world's largest religious society continued to use attitudes which made for an avoidable increase in population on a planet already gravely over-populated, then that concerned everyone whose supply of breathable air and drinkable water and eatable food was threatened as a result."[8]

Although the Catholic Church has every right to establish moral laws for its followers, and it may be seen as an impertinence for a non-Catholic to make such sweeping criticisms, it is not only people outside the Roman Church who believe that the church is wrong on this issue. Many people within the Catholic communion also plead for a more open and flexible approach on the part of the Vatican.

Catholic Spirituality

"O to see ourselves as others see us!" cried the Scottish poet Robert Burns. Others' views of us, however, are not always complimentary, so many of us steer clear of people's candid opinions. Thus, considering the stereotypes that Protestants have of them, it is not surprising that Catholics have not sought out candid Protestant opinions of their spirituality. It is all too simple to dismiss Catholic laity as people ignorant of the truth, blindly following an infallible Pope, to see Catholic spirituality as at best heretical, at worst pagan.

But we should not let prejudice restrict our view of the spiritual richness of the Catholic Church. Something of this heritage may be gleaned from a glimpse of its liturgical life. The emphasis on movement and reverence, the use of color and smell, the importance of ecclesiastical architecture—all this and much more point to a dimension of liturgical style and richness which is usually absent from Protestant worship. Indeed, Protestant communal spirituality, especially evangelical worship, may seem quite naked compared with such a splendidly garbed companion.

Two aspects of Catholic spirituality—the character of Catholic worship and the Catholic understanding of the communion of saints—are particularly worth exploring for what they may teach the rest of the body of Christ.

Catholic Worship. In beginning to look at Catholic worship, we might ask why many people find it so attractive. There are at least three reasons. One we have already alluded to, namely, the aesthetic element, which seems to blend all the other elements into a coherent whole. While Protestant worship is generally dominated by the importance of the Word proclaimed, and everything else seems to be like the launching stages of a rocket that fall away when the rocket is eventually put into orbit, Catholic worship is carefully orchestrated and balanced, with a rhythm and life which many find refreshing and helpful. We must not overlook the fact, of course, that this aspect is not confined to Catholicism—Anglican, Lutheran and Orthodox churches share in this liturgical heritage. But what cannot be denied is that it is a universal mark of Catholicism.

Second, and perhaps of greater import, Rome has realized the importance of the visual in Christian learning and worship experience. Catholicism has shown great pedagogical wisdom—whether intended or not—in making worship a visual sermon.[9] Most of us need external aids, aids which appeal to our senses and serve as ladders to the divine. Although church history alerts us to the danger of an image becoming an idol, or a help becoming an end in itself, ridding worship of all symbols and rituals—as many of the Puritans did in seventeenth-century England—is also a mistake, because these symbols and rituals have their roles in leading people to deeper levels of faith. If exaggerating external worship has been a special danger of Catholicism, minimizing it has been a Protestant failing.

Catholics have long recognized the value of early education. "Give us a child until he is seven," goes the Jesuit maxim, "and you can have him for the rest of his life." During those impressionable years, a lifetime's habits are formed.

A central stress within this pedagogical approach has been regular attendance at the Eucharist. Catholic children are brought up in the context of the liturgy, absorbing the words of the missal and soaking it up so that it becomes the warp and woof of daily living. This may be less so today than it used to be, but it is still an ideal urged on families by parish priests, and it goes a long way toward explaining why the Catholic Church has been able to retain its hold on the young more successfully than Protestant churches.

What is true in education generally is true spiritually too: We move from concrete learning to the abstract. Concentrate only on abstract theological ideas, and some may be led to attain great heights of spiritual wisdom and knowledge, but many less able people will get nowhere. So the framing of suitable symbols to convey God's truth that the lessons may flow from eye to heart is very important.

The third reason many find Catholic worship so attractive is that

Catholicism appears to offer people a security that they do not find in Protestantism. Protestant churches do not seem to offer a faith with the same kind of guarantees that are proffered by the Catholic Church. Many people think that Protestantism is confusing, offering many competing claims for the spiritual life, while they find the Catholic claim to have the divine mystery in a tangible and visible form more compelling. In short, the Catholic Church possesses an authority which, in an uncertain world with many strident and contradictory voices, millions find attractive.

Of course, Catholic worship has changed a great deal since the Second Vatican Council. As a result, in many advanced societies the liturgy does not possess the attraction it once had, but I still think that this threefold shape—the aesthetic, the visual, the underlying authority—is basically accurate. It would be foolish to deny that Protestants can learn much from Catholic worship; indeed, many mainstream Protestant churches have appropriated Catholic elements in order to deepen the quality of their worship. The Tractarian movement of the nineteenth century, which sought to introduce Catholic practices into the Anglican Church, has greatly influenced the Church of England. Evangelical Anglicans have gained a great deal from many of these shared insights, even if they have considered some theologically wrong.

In spite of the obvious values of worship which appeals to the senses and the imagination, some dangers attend such concentration on external criteria. Worship can be aesthetically beautiful and pedagogically inspiring and yet completely and utterly false. We must not confuse sensuous feelings or evocative liturgy with truth. Further, as history readily shows, churches can all too easily move away from the simplicity of the gospel, allowing the faith to be obscured by many elements which speak of mystery and not of Christ. We must remind ourselves that the first Reformers were Roman Catholic Christians who were not the first to bring the gospel to the church. It was there before them, but medieval spirituality so overlaid it with other elements that its clarity was dimmed.

This danger is not, of course, confined to Catholicism, even if it is a particular danger to that communion. Any church can develop traditions, patterns of worship and styles of spirituality which may take the church far from the message of Jesus and the apostolic community. Although the Reformation is past, the task of reformation is never done because religious people often succumb to the temptation to try to improve the gospel.

The Communion of Saints. The second distinctive aspect of Catholic spirituality is its understanding of the communion of saints. This again is characteristic of Rome's theological and historical understanding of itself as the people of God. Included are such giants as St. Francis of Assisi, St. John of the Cross, St. Francis de Sales, St. Catherine of Siena, Thomas à Kempis, St. Teresa of Ávila and many more. Catholic spirituality throbs with the life of the saints, and their teachings are valued clues toward the kind of life that God rewards. The consequence is that Catholicism has a broader base to its spiritual and worshiping life than is usually found in other branches of the Christian church. As the name suggests, Catholicism represents an openness not only to contemporary worship but also to that of the past. Richard McBrien makes the point that many different streams of theology and spirituality feed the river of Catholicism, and that the Catholic believers draw on many different sources for the enrichment of their faith.

Catholic Christians, therefore, are likely to grow up within a spiritual tradition which assumes that the whole of Christian spirituality is important for them. Even if they do not go directly to the teachings of the saints themselves, they are encouraged to see them as *aids* toward spiritual growth, *models* to follow and *pointers* to the quality of life which God expects. Not just figures of the past, they are living members of the communion of saints which embraces heaven and earth. To be a little more precise, the phrase "the communion of saints" has come to mean the ever-present spiritual union between believers and Christ, and through him between the church on earth and the church in heaven. To this day the Catholic Church is firm in its conviction that fellowship exists between the blessed in glory and those who struggle on earth. The Second Vatican

Council's *Dogmatic Constitution on the Church* declares: "For all who belong to Christ, having his Spirit, form one Church and cleave together in him. Therefore the union of the pilgrims with the brethren who have gone to sleep in the peace of Christ is not in the least interrupted." These, therefore, because of their close communion with Christ, intercede for us on earth and place their merits at our disposal. The constitution continues: "The Church has always venerated the saints, especially the Blessed Mother, and has sought their aid."[10]

Pope Paul VI's Credo of 1968 says much the same thing: "We believe in the communion of all the faithful in Christ, those who are pilgrims on earth, the dead who are being purified and the blessed in heaven, all together forming one Church: and we also believe that in this communion the merciful love of God and his saints is ever turning listening ears to our prayers."

The Catholic Christian has, therefore, been nurtured in a fellowship conscious of a spiritual communion greater than this earthly one where the saints are at hand to help. He is encouraged to seek the aid of the saints in glory. A friend once remarked to me that when she prays to her favorite saint, St. Teresa of Ávila, and asks for help, she is not bypassing Jesus at all. She is just seeking the extra help of Teresa in the communion of saints. She insisted: "Just as I will ask you to pray for me, so I will ask St. Teresa. I ask her because she is in heaven and much closer to the Lord than I am. She can explain to him just how I am feeling and what my real needs are."

We cannot pretend that there are not real theological difficulties that Protestant Christians find with this concept of the saints in glory interceding for us. The Reformers had to meet this problem in their day and protested strongly against the implied diminution of Christ's role as mediator. The *Ten Theses of Berne* (1528) declares: "Christ alone died for us, so he is to be worshipped as the only Mediator and Advocate between God the Father and us believers. Therefore to propose the invocation of other mediators and advocates beyond this life is contrary to Scripture."

In 1530 the Lutheran Augsburg Confession put the issue more positively: "The memory of saints may be set before us, that we may

follow their faith and good works according to our calling . . . but the
Scripture teacheth not to invoke the saints or to ask help of the saints
because it propoundeth unto us one Christ, the Mediator, Propitiator,
High Priest and Intercessor." Other Reformation texts argue the same
point, that there is only one mediator and that the invocation of the
saints is a dangerous practice which may take us far from Christ. A
later Protestant text, the second Helvetic Confession, attempts to hold
the two issues in balance. It contends that "God and Christ the
Mediator are sufficient for us (as our intercessors). . . . At the same
time we do not despise the saints or think basely of them. For we
acknowledge them to be living members of Christ and friends of God
who have gloriously overcome the flesh and the world. Hence we love
them as brothers and also honor them, yet not with any kind of
worship but with an honorable opinion of them and just praise of
them. We also imitate them."

At this point we can see that the two great communions are
colliding theologically. The Catholic perspective stresses that the
whole communion of heaven is brought consciously into view when
Catholics pray, and through the intercession of the saints they believe
that their prayers are presented to the Father. On the other hand,
Protestants argue that this looking to the saints compromises the
mediatorial role of Christ. He is our only mediator, and asking the
saints to pray confuses people concerning his proper role.

The way forward cannot be found by Christians handling such
issues in isolation from the other point of view. Honest dialog is
necessary, in which exposure to the other viewpoint is made possible.
Protestants need to be made aware of the positive aspects of the notion
of the communion of saints, which, incidentally, is also a familiar
concept in some non-Roman churches such as the Anglican communion. Protestant Christians are often prone to separate the church of
the past from that of the present. We need to remind ourselves that
the people of God constitute a much bigger fellowship than the
church militant on earth. We enter into the struggles of Christians
who have passed the baton to us, and we are united with them through
our common Savior, Jesus the Lord. In a mystical and, from our

perspective on earth, a wholly mysterious way, our communion with other believers is not eclipsed by death. As the former Archbishop of Canterbury William Temple once put it, "The Church is the only organization which does not lose its members at death."

Catholic Christians, for their part, may need to explore whether prayers to the saints compromise the meaning of the cross. Don't such prayers blur the ministry of Christ to us? Then, aside from the issue of Christ's uniqueness, they ought to question the point of praying to the saints when we may go straight to the throne of grace (Heb 4:14-16). Why do we need to pray to St. Teresa when we can go straight to the Lord? If he is the incarnate Son of God, Son of man and Son of Mary, the one who taught us to call God "Abba," why pray to anyone else? He is all we need, and he is always available.[11]

The Obedient Church
Words like *loyalty, obedience* and *submission* are hardly popular words today. Yet they are part of Catholic vocabulary and speak of an organization which is hierarchical in structure. Everyone is expected to do his work according to his role within the system. Although the Second Vatican Council amended this emphasis, introducing the notion of family, obedience is still a significant word for Catholics. If, then, we wish to have a deeper understanding of Catholicism and to appreciate the tenacity of this church, we have to note the importance of authority and obedience as two of the constituents of the Catholic faith.

The reason for this is not hard to find. As we have observed, the doctrine of the church is not on the outskirts of Catholicism as it is in some forms of Protestantism. It is at the center. This may be observed particularly in the way theology is taught. While Protestant teaching usually develops in the direction Bible/Fathers/church, traditional Catholic theology has proceeded church/Fathers/Bible. What the church teaches is for the Catholic not an optional extra but the center of faith, and it is far more important than what any individual believes.

To Catholics, then, obedience is not a narrowing thing but part of their total obedience to God, of which the papacy is a focus and expression. Perhaps the most celebrated, and possibly the most extreme expression of obedience, is that of St. Ignatius, founder of the Jesuit order, who wrote: "We should put away completely our own opinion and keep our minds ready and eager to give our entire obedience to our Holy Mother the hierarchical Church. . . . To arrive at complete certainty, this is the attitude of mind we should maintain: I will believe the white object I see is black if that should be the decision of the hierarchical Church." Nevertheless, Ignatius was quite prepared to criticize the leadership of the church of his day when the standards of church life fell below what he considered to be the ideal, but he saw this as part of his devotion and love for the church.

Such obedience is traditionally given, not to an abstract church but to those who have the responsibility of governing the people of God. At the pinnacle of this stands the Pope, who is considered to be the Vicar of Christ, Pontifex Maximus, and yet in terms of his ministry "servant of the servants of God." For devout Catholics, the Pope, who is the successor of Peter and heir to his responsibilities and promises, deserves and, as a rule, is given unswerving love and devotion. Through this authority structure, Catholicism reaches into the lives of millions of people. In 1959 Jaroslav Pelikan wrote: "The Roman Catholic is trained to look to his Church not only for guidance and inspiration, but also for direction on how to live, how to work and how to think. Even in a complex modern society the long arm of the Church's power reaches into almost every province of his life."[12]

Compared with that kind of obedience, the average Protestant seems a fair-weather Christian. He shows little such commitment to his own church. If he does not like the minister, the people, the place, he has little hesitation in going elsewhere.

Such loyalty, then, as a characteristic, helps to explain the success of Catholicism in establishing itself throughout the world. It makes the Catholic Church seem like a purposeful army, going into battle with order, dignity and discipline. The obedience of priests to go where sent and of the people to do what they are told has been one of the great marks of Rome. So we can begin to understand older

Catholics who regard unquestioning obedience as a strengthening thing because it creates a harmonious context in which orders are carried out to the letter without challenge or controversy. Two observations must be made on this concept of authority and obedience.

First, obedience to those in authority in the church is a proper biblical insight and command. Paul expected submission to his own authority in the church. As church founder and pastor, his concept of authority was certainly not that of the slave owner, but more like that of a father who desired that his children should grow into mature Christians. He also expected Christians to obey not only him but also all those set over them in the Lord. This concept of respect for those who work among believers and to whom authority is given deserves more attention from Protestant Christians. At the same time, the interaction between authority and obedience cannot be divorced from truth. Those who lead are accountable not only to those above them but also to those whom they lead. Even in family life the authority of parents is never absolute, except when children are very young. As children grow up they expect to see consistency in conduct and conformity between what parents say and what they do. For the teen-ager a precondition of obedience is, naturally enough, the rationality of the instruction. It has to make sense; it must be coherent, clear and intelligible.

Similarly, the dynamic between authority and obedience in church life requires accountability as well as trust, rationality as well as revelation. I think it is true to say that the older Catholic view of absolute obedience has given way over the last twenty years or so to a more questioning attitude toward those in authority. This is due partly to the spirit of change blowing through the church and partly to the influence of the secular world. Catholics are now less likely to obey just because some spiritual superior tells them to. For example, Pope John Paul II has a tremendous following throughout the world. Most people respect his emphasis on human rights and his call for a positive Catholicism. But it is commonly recognized today that his views and those of the Catholic hierarchy on contraception, family life and the role of women, for example, are ignored by possibly 75% of Catholics in the Western world.

There are older Catholics who mourn the passing of the age of absolute obedience, but a better-educated laity cannot be encouraged to take on more responsibilities in the church without allowing them a greater degree of participation in the making of decisions. Many educated Catholics, in fact, find themselves unable to reconcile aspects of the church's teaching with their own knowledge of life. Further, the reluctance of the Vatican to allow discussion in depth on some of these issues has led to the opening of a wide chasm between the hierarchy of the church and ordinary Catholics. This, however, has interesting theological possibilities, because the Catholic Church has always laid great store on how the faithful feel about the spiritual life. This is known as the *sensus fidelium*. The *sensus fidelium* was, in fact, one of the factors which encouraged Pope Pius IX to promulgate the Dogma of Infallibility in 1870. The logic seems to be that if the laity are calling for substantial changes in areas of personal ethics and ecumenism, this modern *sensus fidelium* should be heeded likewise.

A second reflection must surely be on the character of John Paul II. He is an interesting example of how personality and role can affect each other. Perhaps the most colorful and interesting figure to appear on the international scene since the era of Kennedy and Khrushchev, he makes it hard to understand just what his attitude to freedom in the church is. Some view him as a progressive Pope, anxious to build on the openness of his predecessors; others see him as a conservative who wishes the whole church to return to a traditional Catholicism.

On the one hand he is a welcoming, warm and friendly man. He epitomizes a loving Christian minister, in touch with the real interests of humanity, compassionate and kind. He has humanized the papacy in a way that no one, except Pope John XXIII, has done. This humanity is expressed not only in his pastoral manner, but also, more definitively, in his teaching. Two important encyclicals, *Redemptor Hominis* and *Laborem Exercens,* put forth his condemnation of human wrong and oppression.

Redemptor Hominis states that one cannot separate salvation in

Christ from life in the world. Christ is in the world and calls for Christians to get immersed in loving action as he did. *Laborem Exercens* calls all Christians to struggle for justice for working people, recognizing that workers are often alienated from the wealth they produce. "Justice for the working class is linked with justice according to the Gospel. The Church seeks a more just world and all those who share in this struggle walk the way of the Gospel, the way of Christian doctrine." This must be music to the ears of the radical! And even the identity between Christian doctrine and the struggle for justice is striking. It is almost as if he were saying: "If you work for a better world, you are really a Christian."

But this somewhat breathtaking view is strangely incompatible with the other side of the Pope's personality, where the traditional side of his Romanism is expressed. We have to remember that Karol Wojtyla is a Pole. In spite of his deep and extensive education, he has been shaped by a Polish Catholicism well known for its conservatism and emphasis on traditional virtues. He has a deep devotion to the Virgin Mary which is almost inseparably connected with a desire to bring Jesus to all people. Since becoming Pope, he has been untiring in his reiteration of orthodox Catholic teaching and the importance of the Catholic family. He has been heavily criticized for an unmodified traditionalism in matters of family life, in organization of worship, in the context of the faith, in his attitude to women, and toward ecumenism.[13] These and other reactions according to some have indicated that the Pope is to the right of the moral center, making a strange contrast with his person-centered political and social views.

On the other hand, Catholic Christians may respond, there is no contradiction here at all. Pope John Paul II is not suffering from theological schizophrenia but rather seeking to act as supreme pastor to 700,000,000 Catholics. He has assumed office at perhaps the most difficult period in the history of the papacy when human affairs are in full flood and when his church is undergoing its greatest internal upheaval ever. It is a fair point that at such a time the most sensible action is to go for the brakes and not the throttle, to stabilize the church, and this, some will say, is what the Pope is doing.

Yet the question of authority and how decisions are reached brings us full circle to the role of the Pope in the church. Catholic Christians must understand that they cannot simply treat this as a domestic issue if we are seriously to talk about unity. It is our issue and our problem as well. Now, it is accepted that the papacy is a major stumbling block to other churches whose concept of authority is fundamentally different from that of Rome.

Pope Paul VI remarked ruefully in a speech to the Secretariat for Christian Unity in 1967: "The Pope, as we well know, is undoubtedly the greatest obstacle in the path of ecumenism."[14] The issue is not the problem of one man ruling over a united church. There is nothing theologically objectionable about that, any more than one person having ultimate responsibility for one congregation. Many Protestants, indeed, are willing to accept the primacy of the Pope, provided that it is not a dictatorship but a shared leadership with other bishops, the "first among equals." The problem at bottom is the issue of the Pope ruling *de jure*—that is, by divine right—and that his authority is fundamentally different from that of other bishops. Both Orthodox and Protestant churches reject this interpretation, finding little biblical or historical support for the claim.

In a recent and important book, *The Bishop of Rome*, Fr. Jean Tillard, a member of the Anglican-Roman Catholic International Commission, offers another way forward.[15] He agrees that the papacy is a stumbling block to unity and that steps must be taken to resolve the points of tension. His book traces the growth of the papacy from its origins in the New Testament to its key role in the early church and on to its climax in the Medieval Period, which resulted in a "Pope who is more than a Pope—a super-Pope." The First Vatican Council's ruling on the infallibility of the Pope was, he admits, a triumph for the ultramontane party because through it the church was made an extension of the papacy and declared dependent on it. After Vatican I, remarks Fr. Tillard, "there is only one sovereign power in the Church and that sovereignty resides completely in the Vicar of Christ."[16]

The Second Vatican Council led to a significant shift in the church's understanding of the papacy, argues Fr. Tillard, especially in its emphasis on the principle of collegiality—that is, the whole body of bishops governing together under the leadership of the Pope. It also saw the church proceeding from the bishops as "successors of the Apostles" instead of from the Pope alone.

Fr. Tillard contends, however, that Vatican II did not go far enough, because it never settled the difficult question of the boundary between the Pope and the other bishops. It did, however, take one very significant step. Pope Paul VI wanted Chapter 22 of the Constitution *Lumen gentium* to close with a note saying that the Roman Pontiff ought certainly to take account of the collegial power of the bishops, but that "he himself owed account to God alone." The commission replied: "The Roman Pontiff is bound by Revelation itself, the basic structure of the Church, the sacraments, the definitions of the first Councils, etc. It is impossible to list them all."[17] Important as this statement is as clarifying the limits of the Pope's powers, Vatican II's lack of clarity has led to fragile results, according to Fr. Tillard.

Fr. Tillard's suggestion is that the church get back to the character of the papacy as it was in the period of the Great Tradition, the tradition of the seven undisputed councils before the East-West split of A.D. 1054. The papal model in this period is Pope Gregory the Great, whose leadership was that of a lowly servant to the servants of God. Fr. Tillard quotes approvingly Gregory's letter to the Patriarch of Alexandria, who had given Gregory the praiseworthy title of *Universal* Pope. Gregory the Great replied no less warmly, but certainly firmly, "Here at the head of your letter I found the proud title of Universal Pope which I have refused. I pray your most beloved Holiness not to do it again because what is exaggeratingly attributed to another is taken away from you. It is not in words that I find my greatness but in manner of life. My honour is the solid strength of my brothers."[18]

This ancient tradition of the Pope as servant and sentinel of the people of God, Fr. Tillard suggests, should provide the model for the contemporary papacy. This bold and imaginative suggestion would certainly receive the approval of Protestant Christians who could not tolerate a leader who was, by definition, six feet above contradiction. It would also seem to fit in well with the character of leadership as expressed by the Second Vatican Council. It remains to be seen whether John Paul II views his office in these terms and whether a proper dynamic relationship develops between his role and that of the college of bishops.

A Sacramental Fellowship

When the Pope visited Britain in 1982, his planned activities included the seven traditional sacraments of his church. During his six-day visit, he celebrated each of these rites—baptism, reconciliation, confirmation, Holy Communion, marriage, ordination and the anointing of the sick and dying. His actions illustrate, better than mere words can, the importance of the sacraments for the Catholic Christian. The Roman Catholic Pope visits a Protestant country for the first time since the Reformation and celebrates each of the Catholic sacraments!

The casual observer might think that nothing could be more offensive to Protestant sensitivities than the sight of the Pope concentrating on issues which divide, unless one understands that the sacramental is at the heart of being a Catholic. The well-known Catholic theologian Edward Schillebeeckx argues in his book *The Eucharist* that Catholics understand Christian truth quite differently from Protestants.[19] This I think must be acknowledged. Catholics see the whole of life as sacramental, especially the church, God's chosen vehicle of grace. God's life, they believe, comes to us in many varied forms: the grace of life through baptism, the grace of forgiveness through the sacrament of reconciliation, the grace of healing through anointing, the grace of Christ's own presence in Holy Communion, and so on. They picture a vast sacramental fellowship in which God manifests himself through chosen means and ministries. These are the pipes, as it were, through which flow the gifts and graces of God.

Seeing the church as a sacramental fellowship supports, consoles and strengthens Catholics. It is not surprising that so many find it attractive. The rhythm and order of the Christian year in which the sacraments have their place gives security and hope. Like a divine escalator it carries you along. You do not have to think or do much; the sacraments are always there to take you. They offer comprehensive coverage for all the hazards and accidents of life.

This concept contrasts sharply with the Protestant picture of God's world. Our categories tend to be more personal. We think of God, Christ and the Holy Spirit as divine persons within the Trinity offering us life directly. God's grace comes to us, we say, personally. We do not live within the framework of the church as a sacramental reality. This is what Schillebeeckx is getting at in his observation that the differences between Catholics and Protestants concerning the Eucharist go back to a deeper difference concerning our understanding of the spiritual life. The "Catholic" God is immanent in the world, accessible through his chosen priests and channels. The "Protestant" God is transcendent, out there, sovereign, revealing himself to whomever he wishes.

The consequences of this are somewhat surprising. We would have every reason to think on the basis of this analysis that Protestants would stress God's sovereignty and grace, while Catholics would be more human-centered.

This tidy division becomes rather ragged, however, in actual fact. It is all too easy for the Protestant perception of reality, which begins from God's grace, to end in a life of deeds. We may say that the Christian life is based on faith and grace, but in practice it can become human-centered. Take worship in many Protestant traditions. The difference between Catholic and Protestant worship often boils down to the question "Who are you trying to please?" The more active quality of Protestant worship, as contrasted with the more passive expression in Catholicism, may suggest that, although God is the overt center of worship, Protestants spend a great deal of time trying to please the congregation.

Or take the Christian life itself. To a great extent, the Protestant ethic can lead to a human-centered approach which elevates our prowess and glory. As we know, the Protestant ethic was one of the results of the Reformation which freed the individual from the power of the church. No longer bound intellectually, socially and economically, individuals were freed to explore. This is one of the reasons why the scientific spirit was able to flourish under Protestantism, because it allowed free inquiry. The consequent irony was that the principle of salvation by faith alone became coupled very quickly with a work ethic which stressed human glory and ability. In my experience as a pastor and counselor I have met quite a few Christians who have never fully appreciated that the doctrine of free grace should affect them psychologically as well as theologically. So many of them have felt the burden of a Christianity which has demanded results in worship, witness, good works, a holy life, and so on. And this ethical expectation has been uneasily connected with a doctrine which should have been experienced in their hearts as well as their minds.

There are signs today that both great traditions are discovering that truth is to be found in both approaches—the sacramental and the personal—and not in just one alone. Protestantism has surely much to learn from the sacramental approach of the Catholic. This has always been an aspect of Christianity, as we can easily discover from the writings of the church in the early centuries. The tendency of Protestantism, perhaps, has been to ignore the created order as the place where God meets us today. Yet this is what incarnation is all about. God comes to us through natural means. The grace of Jesus is ministered to us, sometimes through channels chosen by God, such as the sacraments, preaching and so on, but at other times through prayer gatherings, Christian fellowship, nature, art and many other ways. Modern Catholicism is gaining much from the biblical insight that grace cannot, and must not, be separated from the personal activity of God, and that the sacramental cannot be restricted to the sacraments ordained by the church.

Our brief look at the distinctiveness of Catholicism is thus over. We have tried to get within this vast communion and have endeavored to assess its strength. I hope Catholic Christians will forgive any observations which are hurtful or overly critical. It is now time to look at the distinctiveness of Protestantism and to consider its strengths and weaknesses.

Chapter 6
PROTESTANT WELLSPRINGS OF FAITH

*W*hat a peculiar lot Protestants must seem to Catholics! At least Catholics can claim to be one church, but Protestants appear to be a confused gaggle of congregations unsure of their real identity. A Muslim once remarked of Christianity that "where you get ten Christians you get eleven different sets of opinion!" He could so easily have been speaking of the Protestant world.

Yet in spite of the variety of Protestant bodies and the differences which exist among them, there is in fact an underlying unity of Christian belief which Roman Catholics, or anyone else who wants to understand the genius of Protestantism, should consider. But first we must deal with the word *Protestant*. It is often thought that the word means someone who protests against the errors of Rome. It has come to acquire mainly that meaning. But, in fact, it means "one who declares something publicly" or "one who makes a solemn declaration." The term is derived from the "Protestatio" of some members of the Diet of Speyer in 1529 who declared their allegiance to the gospel of Christ with a call to the church to return to a biblical Christianity. While it is true that the first Protestants opposed deviations from the gospel, the primary meaning of the term was a positive affirmation of truth as they saw it.[1]

As we have already noted the Reformers had no wish in the beginning to start a new denomination. They belonged to their church and wished to reform it from within. They were proud to be at one and the same time *Catholic* and *reformed* Christians—Catholic, because they belonged to the one holy catholic and apostolic church, and reformed, because their overwhelming desire was for the church to reform itself in the light of the gospel. "We are the church," they declared, "which washed its face at the Reformation." The use of the word *washing* suggests that they did not believe they were adding or subtracting from the church's faith: rather their "Protestation" originated in a drive to restore the church to its original nature and vision.[2]

There are five great Protestant emphases at the heart of mainstream non-Roman churches. I do not claim that all Protestants will acknowledge these factors to be of equal importance. What I do claim, however, is that in this cluster of common emphases we shall feel the pulse of Protestantism. Just as we did in the last chapter, we shall explore these themes from both Catholic and Protestant viewpoints to uncover the points of tension as well as to outline the contribution that Protestantism makes to our understanding of the gospel.[3]

The Finished Work of Jesus

At the time of the Pope's visit to Britain in June 1982, I was struck by the incongruity of two enormous banners held by a Protestant woman outside Westminster Abbey. One said "Down with Popery"; and the other, "Christ died for our sins, the just for the unjust." She stood alongside various entrepreneurs who were offering papal memorabilia for sale. The juxtaposition of the two banners was interesting. Clearly she used the biblical text because she assumed that the Roman Church did not believe that Jesus' death was a full and sufficient atonement for sin. She was, as it happens, quite wrong about this, and we will return to that point later, but she was right to place the emphasis on the cross.

If the New Testament is our guide, we must recognize that the work of Jesus is complete and finished. The uncompromising teaching of Paul is that Christ's atonement is universal in its scope and full in its effect. The same conclusion is reached in the letter to the Hebrews. It argues the once-for-all nature of Christ's sacrifice on the cross. Unlike the high priests of the Old Covenant who offered annual sacrifices for sins, God's own self-offering is unique and unrepeatable. The phrase *once-for-all* is hammered home to reinforce the writer's argument that Christian salvation is final. Christ finished his work and "sat down at the right hand of God." We cannot add to or subtract from what God has done through his Son, the only mediator between God and man.

What Protestantism has tried to do is to be faithful to this New Testament witness concerning the finality and all-sufficiency of Christ. Since the Reformation the two steady emphases have been the total sufficiency of Christ in salvation and the sufficiency of his grace for every kind of need.

The first aspect, *the sufficiency of Christ,* led to the rejection of the notion of mediating priests within the church. Christian ministry is never called priestly in the New Testament. Christ alone is our great high priest, and in a special but analogical way all of us in the Christian body are "priests and kings to God." That is, we are a *royal priesthood* in Christ with a ministry to represent him to the world, to proclaim his forgiveness and to make his love known. The notion of Christian priests offering a sacrifice to God—whether re-presenting or re-offering his sacrifice—is viewed as a denial of the efficacy of his death and a serious break with the tradition of the New Testament apostolic church. The Mass, argued Martin Luther, is not something we offer but something we receive: "I fear that many have made out of the Mass a good work, whereby they thought to do a great service to Almighty God. . . . A testament is not a benefit received but a benefit conferred: it does not derive benefit from us but brings us benefit. Who has ever heard that he who receives an inheritance does a good work? He does derive benefit. Likewise in the Mass, we give Christ nothing but only take from him."[4]

The second emphasis, *the sufficiency of grace*, flows from this. If Christ's death is the basis for our forgiveness, restoration, healing, peace and all the other great benefits of our salvation, then no human being can intervene and bring them to us. They are ours either through Christ or not at all. This is again firmly expressed in Luther's own words: "So we see how great the need and benefit of Christ is to us and recognize the fallacy of the position that one may by his own natural powers earn God's Grace: Yes, recognize it as a device of Satan himself. For if human nature can obtain grace, Christ is unnecessary as an intercessor, a mediator. But he being essential, human nature can obtain only disgrace: the two are inconsistent—Man his own mediator, and Christ the mediator for Man."[5]

All this looks cut and dried, as the woman standing with her banners probably thought. But the situation is more complex than perhaps we realize. To begin with, as far as I can judge, Catholic theology believes and always has that the death of Jesus was a full atonement for sin for all time. The Council of Trent declares: "The meritorious cause [of justification] is his most beloved only begotten, our Lord Jesus Christ, who, when we were enemies, for exceeding charity wherewith he loved us, merited justification for us by his most holy passion on the wood of the cross, and made satisfaction for us unto God the Father."[6] The Second Vatican Council also proclaimed firmly that "our thoughts are concerned first of all with those Christians who openly confess Jesus Christ as God and Lord—as a *sole* mediator between God and man unto the Glory of the only God, Father, Son and Holy Spirit."[7] And more recently the representative theologians of the Anglican-Roman Catholic International Commission (ARCIC) declared in the "Agreed Statement on The Eucharist" that "Christ's redeeming death and resurrection took place once for all in history. Christ's death on the cross, the culmination of his whole life of obedience, was the one perfect and sufficient sacrifice for the sins of the world. There can be no repetition of or addition to what was then accomplished once for all by Christ."[8]

The difficulties do not lie, therefore, in our understanding of the finality of Christ's victory. They lie in our interpretation as to how it is made available to us. The Protestant view is that the work of Christ is applied through the Holy Spirit, through the personal activity of God himself, to all who want to follow Jesus. There is therefore an immediacy about the Protestant position. To the person who wants to find faith, Christ makes his home in his heart. Of course, this takes place within the Christian church and not divorced from it. The idea that this is a pietistic, subjective theology must be rejected once and for all. While non-Christians may begin their search for faith *outside* the church, only through the Christian body or its representatives do they come to faith in Christ and in so doing join the fellowship of God's people. There is nothing individualistic about this. There is in fact something inherently Christ-glorifying about the Protestant position. The emphasis falls on Christ and his deeds. Faith is a transaction between Jesus as Savior and us as sinners. As the hymn puts it, "nothing in my hands I bring, simply to your cross I cling."

Catholics might likely respond that the weakness of the Protestant position is that it tends to ignore the role of the ministry of the church in making Christ's salvation available. There is a proper priesthood in ministry, they might say, which is faithful to the Bible and the early church, and which need not blur the distinctiveness of Christ or minimize his finished work.

However, a clear example of the problem is expressed by the Council of Trent's Statement on the Mass. "And forasmuch as, in this divine sacrifice which is celebrated in the Mass, that same Christ is contained and immolated in an unbloody manner who once offered himself in a bloody manner on the altar of the cross; the holy Synod teaches, that this sacrifice is truly propitiatory, and that by means thereof this is effected, that we obtain mercy. . . . For the victim is one and the same, the same now offering by the ministry of priests, who then offered himself on the cross, the manner alone of offering being different."[9]

This statement, written against the background of the Reformation, sets out a different perspective from that of Protestant belief. To be sure, in examining our views of the Lord's Supper we should not overlook our common starting point in the death of Christ as the basis of our salvation. But the theologies of salvation here are profoundly different. For Protestants the death of Jesus is utterly decisive and final. As a consequence the Mass or Lord's Supper is a sacrament, not a sacrifice; or at the very most it is a sacrifice of praise and thanksgiving and the offering of our lives, but never a propitiatory sacrifice which has a bearing on salvation. For Catholics, on the other hand, the benefits of salvation are made directly available through the Mass, which is considered to be an extension of the cross. Through the ministry of properly ordained priests, the church takes an active role in administering Christ's salvation. The Mass is therefore a sacrament of salvation rather than a sacrament of the gospel: or, to put it another way, it *is* salvation rather than the setting forth of salvation.[10]

In terms of interpreting the means of salvation, the differences are profound. There is obviously much room for fruitful dialog and progress here. If both sides emphasize so clearly the finality of Christ's death for our salvation, both need to explore the areas of difference which separate us. For Protestants the issue may be that of exploring the nature of priesthood and the role of ministers as a sacramental channel. For Catholics the question revolves around the fullness of Christ's salvation and their explicit connection of Calvary with the Mass. But leaving aside the problem of interpretation, the genius of Protestantism rests in its emphasis on the event and the effect of the cross. Consequently, for Protestants Jesus Christ is central, especially in evangelical worship and devotion. If he is the Lord of glory who gave his life for others, then there can be no reluctance to commit ourselves to him or to worship him. He is incomparable and no shadow must darken the light of his presence.

The Bible: Yardstick of Faith and Center of Piety

I make no apology for coming back yet again to the Scriptures, because they are central to the Protestant understanding of the faith and the Christian life. The fervent desire of the Reformers was that the Bible should be available to all people. William Tyndale, the great New Testament translator of the time, said to some of his persecutors:

"If God spares my life, ere many years I will take care that a ploughboy shall know more of the Scriptures than you do."

There was a twofold reason for this aim. The first was that Scripture, once it was known, loved and rooted in the heart of the church, would clearly be the yardstick of Christian teaching. The second was more important for Reformers like Tyndale—he wanted Scripture to root itself in the hearts of individuals, becoming the inspiring center of devotion and heartbeat of conduct. Perhaps Tyndale's dream of the Bible in every heart and every home has not been fulfilled as well as he would have liked. Nevertheless, even today wherever a sturdy Protestant faith thrives, you will find Bible-loving Christians who preach it, teach it and live by it. It is the basis of Protestant spirituality and the oasis of devotional life.

As we have already considered, both traditions have grown together greatly in attitudes toward the Bible. We agree that it is the root of Christianity—where else can we look for a standard to measure what is true or false? Unlike most human activities and beliefs, which might grow *out of* old knowledge, leaving the original behind like a discarded kernel, Christianity is an organism which grows *from* New Testament faith and in conformity with it.

There are, however, uncomfortable questions which some Christians will present to Protestants who stress the authority of Scripture in the Christian life.[11] Isn't it a fact, they say, that this tendency unleashes a pious subjectivism? A criticism of some weight is that Protestants argue strongly for the clarity of Scripture yet seem unable to agree as to what it actually teaches or means. The result is further division in the body of Christ.

We must agree that the Bible may be twisted and certain teachings either exaggerated or ignored. The texts of Scripture can be used to support many different things, as history readily shows. To this day, mainstream churches and offbeat sects all claim the Bible to be their source of authority but sometimes use it in contradictory ways. And yet this problem, which we acknowledge freely, can easily be exaggerated. In fact, there are great areas of agreement among Protestant denominations concerning the interpretation of Scripture.

There may be differences here and there, but on the whole the variations are surprisingly few. Neither should we overlook the fact that the differences can be as wide within a tradition as between traditions.

But neither breadth of interpretation nor misuse of Scripture should lead us to minimize its importance for Christian truth. The Bible has a central role in the life of the Church as an authority and guide. It is our unique and fundamental authority. Nevertheless, Protestants would do well to grow in their appreciation of the role of tradition in our discovery of God's truth. Tradition is like an individual's personal history. Our experience can help us make wise decisions and judgments. Christian tradition, where it is genuine and true, will not go against Scripture but will draw out and confirm its teaching. And, on the other side, reliable church tradition will grow out of faithfulness to the teaching of Scripture. Ultimately, tradition must be subject to Scripture, as Protestants have affirmed, but Protestants have often overlooked the positive contribution that tradition can and does make to our understanding of Scripture. Moreover, they have often been blind to the impact that their own Protestant tradition has in their interpretation of Scripture.

The interpretation of the Bible requires a mature and intelligent faith to make its greatest impact. Evangelical Christians, especially, have been guilty of treating the Bible in a simplistic fashion, ignoring the historical, literary and cultural dimensions of this greatest of all books. We have been inclined to use it as a kind of *Old Moore's Almanac* to which one goes to select a promise, a gift or a blessed thought. This is not to deny that God speaks through it and uses individual verses of Scripture to challenge and help us. Indeed not. But as a general rule Scripture has first to be interpreted in its original context before we apply it to ourselves.

So there are dangers involved in the use of the Bible in the church, and this I freely admit. Nevertheless, because the Bible is God's book, it points to the truth in Jesus and will take us to him if we allow it to. Charles Spurgeon, that great Baptist preacher in the last century, replied to the call that we needed to protect the Bible against the attacks of atheists: "Defend the Bible, sir? I would sooner defend a lion!" And a lion it is, well able to look after itself.

This strong emphasis on the place of Scripture in the life of the Christian is one of the great springs from which Protestantism rises. The Bible, as Pope Gregory the Great said so long ago, is "a kind of river both shallow and deep, in which the lambs may find a footing and the elephant float at large." Protestants who are true to their tradition treasure Scripture as God's written Word to his people and the spiritual center of their walk with God. Here, as we have already observed, is a thrilling opportunity for greater unity, because Catholic Christians are being encouraged to discover the spiritual resources and truths of Scripture. How much better for us to do this together!

A Personal Faith

In our growing knowledge of one another, Catholics need to understand that the personal relationship many Protestant Christians, especially evangelicals, claim to have with Jesus is not an arrogant, individualistic piety, but a humble experience of God's grace. Other Christians have found claims to this type of Christian experience threatening and perhaps even distasteful. Many people have echoed Bishop Butler's condemnation of John Wesley's profession of a personal knowledge of Christ: "Pretending to extraordinary revelations and gifts of the Holy Ghost is a horrid thing—a very horrid thing."

The evangelical or charismatic experience of new life often differs from that of other Christian people, especially in the area of assurance. Some people see the Christian life as a road which takes them to God, a road along which there is no complete assurance. So, to the direct question "Do you know God?" they might reply, "Well, I think I do. I go to church and receive the help and ministry it gives. But I cannot lay claim to any certainty." Or to the question "Are you secure in the Christian hope of everlasting life?" the same person might answer with some hesitancy, "I hope so." Such cautious responses seem lame and imprecise alongside the evangelical conviction that we can know that we are forgiven, that we can know God, that

Christ holds us firmly and will never let go.

The Roman Catholic theologian Avery Dulles mentions in one of his books that he was impressed one day by a young Protestant Christian who shared with Dulles the story of how he experienced a personal conversion to Jesus as his Savior. Since that event, the young man explained, he had made it his chief business to witness and preach about his Lord. Dulles was struck by the thought that many thousands of young Protestants are spreading their faith like that young man, and he wondered how many Catholics could do the same.[12]

Yet it was precisely this sort of confidence that Catholics at the time of the Reformation were suspicious about. The Council of Trent rejected what it believed to be the somewhat arrogant and self-confident faith of the Protestants. It declared: "For even as no pious person ought to doubt of the mercy of God, of the merit of Christ, and of the virtue and efficacy of the sacraments, even so each one, when he regards himself, and his own weakness and indisposition, may have fear and apprehension touching his own grace; seeing that no one can know with a certainty of faith, which cannot be subject to error, that he has obtained the grace of God."[13]

With the advantage of hindsight we can see that both Protestants and Catholics were not able to appreciate the insight of the other. Certainly the Reformers were not basing their assurance of salvation on subjective experience but rather on the mercies and promises of God. Indeed, the Reformers would have wholeheartedly agreed with Trent's statement *"On the gift of Perseverance"* that "all ought to place and repose a most firm hope in God's help."[14] An arrogant, self-assured faith was far from their thought. To them the nature of justification as a declaration of acquittal implied a God-given certainty of one's own pardon and salvation.

To this day the evangelical emphasis on personal faith arouses suspicion. Yet, evangelical Protestants claim, this emphasis is firmly rooted in Scripture, Christian history and experience. Take the experience of New Testament Christians, and we will be impressed by the infectious quality of a personal faith. Peter, preaching on the day of Pentecost, had no lack of assurance or certainty. He assumed that

Jesus could be known and that his grace could be experienced. As a result three thousand people responded and were baptized. Again, when Philip met the Ethiopian eunuch on a desert road there was no equivocation, no apologetic "it may be that my faith has a bearing on your situation." Philip, we read, preached Jesus. The man responded and sealed his commitment in baptism. The New Testament throbs with that kind of immediate, personal faith. There can be no denying this.

The Reformers' emphasis on this kind of certainty constituted a radical challenge to the priestly, sacramental understanding of grace current in the church of their time. Reacting against the Reformers, Roman Catholic theologians took up positions which seemed to exclude any certainty of experiencing the grace of God. Thus there emerged the ironic and paradoxical picture of the Church of Rome, which believed in the theory of justifying grace transforming a person and giving new life, now attacking the notion that we can be confident in the word of hope. As F. Clark notes, "The Council of Trent created a climate of opinion unfavourable to any assertion of experiencing divine grace."

Nevertheless, Catholic spirituality did not advocate a life of uncertainty. Clark continues, "Orthodox Roman Catholic belief did encourage the faithful to have a well-favoured hope that they were on the way to salvation. Although absolute certainty was ruled out there were many valid signs in the life of the believer which could give a kind of conjectural assurance that he was not an enemy of God."[15]

Many Catholic theologians recognize today that the language of Trent, framed polemically to define Catholic truth against Protestant "errors," needs to be balanced by a firm doctrine of the reality of our sonship in Christ. They also agree that Christ's victory over sin and death should not result in feebleness or uncertainty regarding the hope of salvation. Trust in the completeness of that triumph can only lead to believers' confidence in the power of their Lord to keep them in the way of faith. The Christian doctrine of assurance is, therefore, not a triumphalistic trust in one's own strength but a firm confidence in God.

This concept of trust in God's promises is central to Protestant, and especially evangelical, spirituality. It is regrettable that from time to time we Protestants make it seem as if our faith and our experience are the ground of our confidence, rather than the promises of God. But it is good to note that this strong, spiritual perspective, which upholds the declaration of Scripture concerning the surety of our sonship in Christ, is not only something we may share with other Christians but something which may also be enriched by their contributions. From the Catholic side Protestants may gain the understanding that to belong to Christ is also to belong to the church and be nourished by it. From the charismatic direction others are reminded not to exclude the Holy Spirit from the experience and expression of conversion. The Holy Spirit lives within those who belong to Jesus, and the gift and graces of the Spirit, in all their exciting variations, are available to all.

Fellowship of Believers

Another specific Protestant contribution to Christianity is its understanding of the nature of Christian fellowship. The Reformation gave birth to the notion of the church as a fellowship of people who share a common faith in Jesus Christ. While the Catholic Church was, and to a great extent still is, a hierarchical church with an emphasis on Christians dwelling in the church and receiving God's grace through lawfully appointed priests and officials, the Protestant churches drew their inspiration from loyalty to the gospel. This contrast was bound to affect people's understanding of the church.

The full consequences of this were not seen during the Reformation. It was not the Reformers' intent to start separate churches; indeed, visible unity was important to them. Their aim was to restore the church to its original rootage in Christ. When this became impossible, national Protestant churches were founded that were based on the authority of Scripture. Martin Luther, for example, defined the church as follows: "Where God's word is purely taught, there is also the upright and true Church."[16]

The problem was this: What did "pure teaching" mean? Protestant

Christians did not find it easy to give a satisfactory answer to this question and the result was twofold. First, further division occurred because some Christian groups such as the Anabaptists did not believe the Reformation had gone far enough. Second, the concept of faith in Christ as the hallmark of a Christian led to ambivalence about the place of the church and sacraments in the Christian life. While for Catholics these were, and are, intrinsic to the Christian faith, to Protestants, by and large, they were considered extrinsic. In other words, while Protestants did not deny the importance of the church and its sacraments, they argued that it was not possible to say who is, or who is not, a Christian simply by whether or not they have been baptized or are members of a particular church.

Evangelical Protestants have taken this a step further. Emphasizing, as they do, the centrality of the death of Jesus and the need to put our trust in him for salvation, they view Christian fellowship in relation to one's response to Christ. If you have accepted Jesus as your personal savior, then you belong to Christ's church regardless of denomination. Illustrative of this in Britain is the famous Keswick Convention in the town of that name. Thousands of Christians come together annually for two weeks in the summer to hear leading evangelicals give Bible expositions. They represent all denominations, and they see their unity not in any one view of the church but in Christ. Indeed, they represent many different shades of opinion on baptism, the Lord's Supper, bishops, church government and the like, but these issues would be considered secondary to the faith they share in Christ. Indeed, the banner over the entrance to the central marquee says it all: "All one in Christ Jesus."

That makes Christianity very attractive and simple—straightforward brotherhood is established on the basis of clear-cut faith in Jesus. But this position has both strengths and weaknesses. Its strength is the centrality of faith in Christ as the hallmark of Christians. This emphasis on faith in Christ above all other matters made evangelicals the first ecumenists. Long before there were broader calls for Christian unity, those who shared an evangelical faith were quick to scramble out of their dugouts and embrace one another. The renewal movement today expresses the same tendency to get behind various church traditions to the faith we have in common. Attend a renewal meeting and you will observe that church affiliation is put quietly aside as Christians worship their common Lord: Catholics, Protestants and Orthodox, all finding that the ground before the cross is level and that the Spirit does not dispense his gifts according to our ecclesiastical pedigree.

But there is a certain weakness in this tendency as well. It is all very well sharing a common faith and sheltering under texts like "All one in Christ Jesus," but, oddly enough, focusing on faith alone can easily lead to an indifference to Christian disunity and apathy about unity. If I retreat into the subjective and rather specious unity I have with like-minded Christians, what about Christians I don't get on with? This subjective emphasis may also lead to a lack of interest in theological truth; hard thinking about unpleasant matters may be replaced by simple pietism.

A devout Christian woman once remarked to me about Christian unity, "Surely we don't need to bother about theology. If you love Jesus, that's all that matters." One gladly wants to affirm the importance of a simple, believing trust in Christ, but the problem with that kind of remark is not that it is simple but that it is simplistic. I am all for a simple, uncomplicated faith in Jesus—the world is crying out for that—but we should all beware of a simplistic faith which brushes aside real problems. The fact is that my faith cannot be separated from the tradition in which it is bred. That tradition comes out of a history in which truth and error, love and hatred, faith and suspicion intermingle.

While it is important to recognize what we have in common with other Christians and do all we can to build bridges into one another's camps, we must recognize that the church of Jesus Christ is not simply a spiritual brotherhood which somehow binds people together independent of organized Christianity. The New Testament does not teach this. The church of Jesus Christ according to the New Testament is the church in Philippi, Rome and elsewhere. It is the body you join by faith and baptism. In other words, belonging to the church is more than simply believing in Jesus. That is, the outward (the belonging, the going, the doing) and the inward (the believing and the trusting) go together.[17]

There is, of course, another problem with the tendency to seek out associations with only like-minded Christians of our own or other denominations. And that is the tendency to create yet more denominations in trying to recapture the purity of New Testament faith. It is a little ironic, as well as sad, that evangelical Christians have separated from one another because of deeply held convictions. Somehow that common faith in Jesus as Savior has not always been a sufficiently strong glue to keep them together. The greater irony of evangelicalism is that while they were likely the first ecumenists, their convictions tend to make them schismatics as well.

What we argue from this is that faith cannot be isolated from the organized church. We may criticize the church—one placard in a demonstration read "Jesus Yes, the church No"—but it is oversimplistic to think of the real church as a kind of overarching, spiritual secret society. The Lord does indeed "know those who are his," but when the books are opened, we may well be confounded by discovering who have been his all along. I think we shall find that he takes the church— that is, the organized reality—more seriously than we think and that his power is at work in it, in spite of its weakness, sin and ambiguity.

The great strength of the Protestant understanding of Christian fellowship, therefore, has to be balanced with the concept of the church as a body in history and society. But the Protestant understanding of the inner unity and fellowship we *already* possess in Christ has an important bearing on modern-day ecumenism, reminding us that unity schemes may resemble the marriage of corpses if the Spirit of life is not already in the churches which desire union.

Priority of Evangelism

Missionary activity has always been a concern of the Christian church, although it has not always been at the forefront of its life and thought. Catholics and Protestants alike have engaged in missionary outreach, and those in both traditions desire to see the whole globe Christianized. But there are differences in approach between Catholics and evangelical Protestants. How serious are they?

The issue was spotlighted for me a few years ago when a number of church leaders in northeastern England met to discuss the possibility of engaging in outreach in our area. An Anglo-Catholic colleague announced that, although he was in sympathy with the desire to share the Christian faith, he felt that his own understanding of evangelism was incompatible with evangelical doctrine. He went on to explain what he understood to be the Catholic doctrine of evangelism. It was, he said, inviting people to join the Christian church and to share in its sacramental life. He did not look for startling conversions or professions of faith, which he considered to be man-centered, but looked rather for God's grace working within the church. For him Christianity was a pilgrimage, a journey, while, as he saw it, the evangelical message was a discovery which was immediate and decisive.

To some degree he was correct in his observations. The classic evangelical understanding of evangelism, which incidentally is not shared by all Protestants, is that God is known through Jesus Christ and that following repentance a new relationship with God begins. The evangelical gospel is a gospel of conversion: through acceptance of Christ and the benefits of his cross and resurrection, a new life commences with the Holy Spirit indwelling the new believer. An attractive simplicity in this teaching is thus one of the cardinal reasons for its success. This tradition has given the world its great evangelists—Wesley, Moody, Torrey, Sunday, Campbell, Graham—to name but a few of the giants. Such men have not stood outside New Testament Christianity as maverick Christians but firmly within it. They share its faith that Jesus Christ is Lord and that his life and death and resurrection demand a response from all. Evangelicals thus have been a strong force in evangelism, the urgency of their message making them notably effective.

But what are the reasons other Christians do not feel they can wholeheartedly agree with the evangelical approach? One reason is that it seems to come with a ready-made answer to all of life's problems, assuming that "if Jesus met my need, he can do exactly the same for you." In other words, the individuality of our situation seems to be obliterated by mass-production line Christianity.

There is truth in this criticism. Evangelicals and charismatics are often guilty of universalizing their own experiences, with the result that some people have been disillusioned when their experience of faith does not quite match the shining examples given. Before we condemn that tendency, however, let us remind ourselves that we shall be condemning the apostle Peter also if we go all the way with this criticism. On the day of Pentecost he preached Christ and made assertions that were nothing short of what a modern evangelist would be proud to say! Perhaps we should infer from this that modern Christians should be eager to preach Christ but should remember that the gospel must be applied personally to individual needs as well as broadcast to the winds.

A second criticism of evangelical preaching is that it neglects real questions with its ready and easy assumption that Jesus Christ is the way. To our announcement that Jesus is the answer, many reply, "Yes, but what is the question?" It is all too easy to present Christianity as the panacea for all ills, to make sweeping statements which brush aside real problems in society and politics.

Naive, arrogant preaching does more harm than good—on this we can all agree—but we should not confuse simplism with simplicity. Simplistic preaching ignores problems and undermines the intellect. Simple preaching comes with humility, eager to share what has been experienced of life in Christ. We ought not to be ashamed of this.

A third reason people are suspicious of such evangelism is that it appears to be a religious version of "cowboys and Injuns"—zealous Christians descend on a district, ignoring its culture and traditions, and preach Christ, taking a few scalps before disappearing over the horizon with their hallelujahs. A lot of evangelism has that kind of quality. And to be fair, where people are well prepared, where churches are involved and where the ground has been effectively tilled, that kind of mass evangelism can be successful. But often it is not, because it does not come from within the culture and situation but is rather a message from the outside hastily grafted onto it.

I witnessed an example of this in 1981. A group of Christians descended on the market square in Durham one Saturday morning just when the market area was crowded with shoppers. The group sang lustily and preached. Their zeal and courage were admirable. Their message was good, clear and true. But, because it was an invasion by an outside group, it was about as effective as a group of aborigines from Australia might have been in proclaiming their beliefs.

Jesus' example suggests that all proclamation should be incarnational; that is, wherever possible the good news should be lived in society before it is merely preached. This must not be taken to mean that the direct method is inappropriate—far from it. Perhaps never before in history has society more needed to hear the gospel of Christ preached clearly and simply. Nevertheless hit-and-run methods are not generally successful in modern culture, because they are external to the life of the community. "Earth it—then disperse it" may be a more biblical way.

Still, evangelicals in their commitment to sharing faith in Christ have an important contribution to make to the wider church fellowship. And as Christians grapple with the urgent task of communicating the good news of Christ, we may hope that the message of reconciliation will draw us together.

In these five aspects we have examined some of the central features of Protestantism. If this has been a more critical chapter than the previous one, it is because as a Protestant, evangelical Christian I have tried to see the weaknesses and strengths of my own tradition. But without doubt the contribution that Protestantism, and within it evangelicalism, can make to wider Christianity is enormous. To dismiss it or brush it aside—or for that matter to do so to the Catholic faith—is to deny an important aspect of the fullness of the faith.

Yet this question of acceptance takes us to the heart of the problem facing many young Christians today: *Where* can I find the true church of Jesus Christ? *What* are the criteria by which I deal with the problems of church membership? *Why* shouldn't I just simply continue in the church in which my parents brought me up?

Chapter 7
ALL AT SEA?

W e left the last chapter with three important questions which reduce to this: if we have honestly been able to appreciate the strengths and weaknesses of the two main Western traditions, by what criteria do we judge where our spiritual home should be?

Two important factors bear on this question. First, the uncertainty and confusion of the churches have resulted in lack of confidence in institutional religion in general. There can be little doubt that the church universal has gone, and is going, through a time of upheaval and revolution almost without parallel. Strange things are happening to the church, events which some Christians find very disturbing and frightening and others find exciting and liberating.

For the first group, the shaking of the foundations has led to the loss of the old securities. The shaking, of course, has been most severe in the Catholic Church, which has had to cope with immense change since the Second Vatican Council. It says a great deal for the resilience of that communion that it has, by and large, remained intact in spite of many problems which could have led to fragmentation and division. Among the issues Catholics have confronted are the replacement of the Latin Tridentine Mass by modern services in the language of the people; moral questions forced on the church by secularism; a theological pluralism represented by Archbishop Lefebre, a traditionalist, on the one hand, and theologians such as Schillebeeckx, Küng and Pohier, on the other hand, whose teachings are much more open and modern. Even though there has been a creative theological response to these issues, there has also been an alarming number of people leaving the church, priests as well as laity, with comparatively few people seeking vocations within it.[1]

Although Protestant churches have not had to face such momentous changes, they have not been immune to the secularization which has hit every religious group. Some denominations have suffered dramatic drops in membership while others have suffered in other ways—loss of confidence in the message of the church and lack of commitment to its work.[2]

For others, however, the shaking of the foundations is exciting and liberating, offering new opportunities for the Spirit of God to bring order out of chaos. Indeed, not all Christian groups have declined in influence and membership. Research has shown that churches which proclaim a simple, direct message about Jesus as Savior and Lord, with confidence and clarity, have grown—in some cases, greatly. But the denominations which have had the most dramatic success are the Pentecostal. Their spontaneous worship, theology of the Spirit and emphasis on the gifts of the Spirit have made them attractive to many. In the wake of Pentecostalism the charismatic movement has penetrated the mainstream denominations, disturbing the structures as well as bringing new insights to the churches. Although this movement has sometimes divided fellowships and in some cases resulted in pietism and exclusivism, it has deepened the life, fellowship and evangelism of many congregations, and its positive contributions should not be denied. As the only renewal in church history, as far as I am aware, to draw Catholics and evangelicals together into a deep harmony in the Spirit, the charismatic movement has had profound effects on Christian unity.

Catapulted by the same social flux, especially in the States and

Britain, the house church movement has sprung into being. The term *house church* is inaccurate as far as the majority of these fellowships are concerned, because they are too large to meet in a home. Their common identity lies in a rejection of institutional religion, which they believe inhibits the Spirit's work in the church and the world. They also share a desire to return to the purity of New Testament faith and practice. Many Christians in the other churches have condemned the house church movement; some believe it to be another unnecessary schism while others accuse it of being world-rejecting, pietistic or fundamentalist. What we need to ask, however, is not where are they wrong but where are they right. The biblical perspective they have grasped and are seeking to put into practice—not in every case to be sure—is that fellowship and ministry must reach into the very depths of the body of Christ.

Jürgen Moltmann touches on this in his book *The Open Church.*[3] He claims that the future of the Reformation does not lie on the right wing of its Catholic tendencies but on the so-called left wing of the Reformation, with the *Schwärmer,* Baptists and sectarians who sought the most radical reformation. Moltmann points out that after a reformation of the faith they wanted a reformation of life through the gathering of the congregation. They were rejected by both Catholics and other Protestants, and many were persecuted. Moltmann asserts that the future of the church lies on this wing of the Reformation "because the widely unknown and uninhabited land of 'the congregation' is found here."

The second factor that bears on our choice of a church home is our understanding of the relation between the kingdom of God and the church. The church is important but the fundamental reality which God is concerned about is the kingdom.[4] In essence the kingdom is the rule or reign of God in the lives of men and women. Teaching about the kingdom was at the heart of Jesus' message. He taught that wherever he is or whenever his words are accepted, the kingdom is there. The kingdom comes into being whenever and wherever people love him and love one another in him. Although Jesus anticipated the coming church by drawing his disciples around him and giving them his commission to proclaim him, his gaze was on the coming of the kingdom. The church then in relation to the kingdom always comes second. The church exists to promote and proclaim the kingdom. The church is faithful or unfaithful insofar as it is a sign and instrument of God's kingdom.

The trap Roman Catholicism fell into was to equate the kingdom with the Catholic Church, so that all members of the church were automatically members of the kingdom of heaven and all others were excluded. The ecclesiology of Vatican II broke with such triumphalism, acknowledging that the role of the church is to witness to the kingdom; the church is a pilgrim community called to manifest Christ to the world.

This definition is one I would want to echo. The church is that community which gives public acknowledgment that the kingdom is among us and continues to grow as Christ is accepted and his teaching lived out. One of our greatest needs today, however, is to recover a biblical vision of the kingdom of God. We have lost Jesus' wider vision of the ultimate victory of God's kingdom. We have become lost in lesser goals like church membership, financial targets, efficient administration and ministerial status. Little wonder Christians are disillusioned!

But if it is impossible to identify the kingdom with any institutional body, neither can we identify the body of Christ with any human organization. Modern Catholic theologians also accept this, agreeing that the church of Christ consists of all those who acknowledge his lordship over their lives. Nevertheless, the official position is still that the fullness of the church *subsists* in the Catholic Church, even though other churches are properly affirmed. The statement is not without its difficulty for Protestant Christians because it implies that Catholicism is somehow more *church* than others and has more truth than the rest. Yet we must not think that equating the body of Christ with its own tradition is a uniquely Catholic fault. Some Protestant groups as well tend to claim absolute positions for themselves, that they alone are "faithful to God's Word," the "remnant" and so on.

All this makes it confusing, especially for young or new Christians, to work out a doctrine of the church that will help them to make wise judgments concerning church membership. If none can claim to be *the* church of Christ, does it matter in fact where we worship? Are there no criteria to bear in mind? It seems as if we have drifted toward a dangerous indifferentism toward the church, seeming to say in the words of Lewis Carroll, "All have won and all shall have prizes."

But, no, there is no need to lapse into despair, apathy or cynicism about the church. There are criteria we can keep before us as we seek a church home. And where better to go than to the ancient notes on the church as one holy catholic and apostolic. These seem to embody the richness as well as the variegated beauty of the body of Christ. We shall study them in the reverse order of the traditional formulation.

An Apostolic Community
If the church is not in the eyes of God the primary reality, it is important, nevertheless, as the community of God's people, and its apostolic function is to proclaim the person and the presence of the king.

Now the word *apostolic* when used of the church may be used in a number of different senses. In its most important and primary meaning we must ask of a particular church or denomination, Is it faithful to apostolic teaching? There is no other saving gospel except the message preached by the apostles and no other Jesus Christ than the one they knew and made known to others. Faithfulness to their testimony recorded in the New Testament is an essential mark of a true continuity in the faith. I must ask about a church, therefore, Do I find in its preaching, practice and life the authentic voice of the New Testament in its witness to Jesus? Does it encourage its members to pay attention to Scripture and to root their spiritual lives there?

There are two recurrent dangers in Christian history. The first is one that Catholic Christians are prone to, namely, to identify apostolicity with succession in ministry, claiming that the only valid ministry is that of the continuity of ministry from Peter down the centuries through the laying on of hands. The only succession the New Testament knows about, however, is the succession of belief and proclamation of the gospel of Christ. "Take the teachings that you heard me proclaim in the presence of many witnesses, and entrust them to reliable people, who will be able to teach others also" (2 Tim 2:2 TEV). It is absolutely true that in this verse Paul has in mind the continuity of ministry, but the reason for it is so that the apostolic message may be handed on.

A similar danger for Protestants from time to time is to assume simply because a Protestant church claims to be biblical, that it is. It does not follow that a church which proclaims Bible texts is necessarily an apostolic fellowship. It may misappropriate Scripture, teach a distorted gospel, or proclaim a narrow, otherworldly pietism which avoids the claims of justice and the cost of apostolic witness. And all this can be done while still claiming to be biblical. The Jehovah's Witnesses, after all, contend that they are faithful to the Bible.

A second meaning of the word *apostolic* when used of the church is that Christ's body is called to manifest the life and ministry of Jesus Christ here and now. Although the concept of apostolic succession—the idea that we can trace a priestly ministry of the church back to Peter—is of dubious historicity, we can properly hold on to a central idea in this notion, namely, that the church today is in continuity with the New Testament body of believers. The church today is, in fact, the New Testament church called to apostolic ministry. The New Testament era is not over; we are in it. To acknowledge this means to take historical continuity seriously. The church has often been disobedient and unfaithful in times past, but God has never deserted his people. His Spirit has not left it completely. Protestants who believe that during the so-called Dark Ages the church was apostate and Spirit-less must account for the fact that this same church preserved the Scriptures, faithfully copying them and holding them for generations to come. It also kept the faith alive through times of persecution and apostasy. The church in every age, indeed, is called not to deny what former generations have given but to hand on truths received, especially the new covenant of God's love in Christ.

To assert this means to take seriously the notion of the church as

Christ's own body fashioned to serve him and love him. Although the shape of ministries such as pastor, teacher, prophet, bishop and deacon may be seen in the New Testament, there is no clear demarcation between clergy and laity. In fact, the only lines of demarcation are functional not essential. The only unique ministerial group in the New Testament is the twelve Apostles whose distinctiveness lay in being witnesses to Christ's resurrection.

However, the same Spirit who empowered them for service empowers and equips everyone else in the body of Christ. Each person as a result has a ministry to offer because he or she has a gift to share. To that extent every Christian participates in apostolic ministry. To be sure, the gifts may vary in their apparent importance. A person may be a finger, an ear, a toe or an arm—to use Paul's analogy of the body—but in God's sight all of us are of equal value because the gifts flow from his Spirit. Another factor which makes the gifts apostolic is that their proper use is never selfish but always for the upbuilding of the church and the extension of the kingdom.

The description of the church as an apostolic body will, then, be a useful guide as we seek to discover where we should settle down as Christians. We will know that we cannot belong to a church which denies the lordship of Christ, or which does not accept his full divinity or the completeness of his salvation, or which does not accept the revelation of Scripture. For that matter, the opportunity for the exercise of our gifts will play an important role too. If our abilities cannot find a proper outlet in a particular fellowship, this may indicate that we have not found the right place. We need to make use of our apostolic talents and gifts in God's service. For example, a church so clerical that it allows little place for the gifts of its members, except in carefully delineated areas, deviates from New Testament Christianity in refusing to recognize the apostolicity of the whole body. This is not necessarily a Catholic failing only; many Protestant fellowships draw rigid barriers between the ministry of the leaders and that of the congregation. I am not, of course, decrying proper structures or attacking the authority of leaders. What I am saying is that if a church cannot make room for the gifts of its members in its worship, witness and service, it will be a disobedient and probably weak community. And probably not one to help young Christians grow.

A Catholic Community

The word *catholic* is a strange word to Protestant ears. Because of its associations with *Roman* Catholicism, it is often avoided as a term to describe the church. But this is a mistake. The word is rich in meaning, and it helpfully outlines the character of the church of Jesus Christ.

The first occurrence of the word *catholic* is in Ignatius's letter to the Smyrnaeans written quite early in the second century. Ignatius, Bishop of Antioch, was on his way to face martyrdom in Rome and on his journey wrote farewell letters to a number of churches urging them to maintain the unity of the church in Asia Minor against the inroads of heretics. Ignatius wrote, "Wherever the bishop is, the congregation should be, just as where Jesus Christ is, there is the catholic church." In this context he meant the whole world, in contrast to the local community for whom the bishop was the center and symbol of unity. It is interesting that in this first use of the word, Christology is at the heart of catholicity. A church that is catholic has Jesus at its center. Indeed, "All one in Christ Jesus" could well be the biblical text for the catholicity of the church, because it stands for the variegated nature of the body in its geographical expansion, numerical size and cultural differences.

In time, however, with the rise of heretical sects the word *catholic* began to lose its meaning of "directed toward the whole" and gradually became a technical term to denote the orthodox church. So the catholic faith meant the orthodox faith of the great churches of Rome, Alexandria, Jerusalem, Antioch and Constantinople. A catholic Christian was one who was in fellowship with the catholic faith of such churches.

Later the idea of fullness was added to its meaning to express the notion that the catholic church was where the fullness of the faith was to be found. The ecclesiology of the pre-Vatican II Church presented this viewpoint. Joachim Salaverri's *De Ecclesia Christi* asserts that "the Roman Catholic Church is the true Church of Christ. This Church alone possesses the notes of unity, holiness, catholicity and apostolicity. All other churches insofar as they lack one or more of these notes are 'false' churches." With such narrowing of the term *catholic* we may see again how a term which is dynamic and inclusive in its basic meaning gradually came to denote something static and exclusive.

If then the catholicity of the church expresses the all-embracing nature of a fellowship of which Christ is the center, what does this actually mean in practice and what might it mean for us today? There are at least two great challenges which it presents, and they extend to Catholics and Protestants alike. The first is a call to commitment to an open Christianity, and the second flows from it as a challenge for Christians to embrace the true catholicism of the faith.

First, a church that is truly catholic is going to express openness by a readiness to make room for all types of people. In the New Testament we find that the only natural ground for dividing the church into separate groups is geographical. Our present-day tendency for churches to be limited to one ethnic group or another denies the catholicity of the faith; it limits our fellowship to "our" people only. This is clear-cut enough, and the majority of Christians would disapprove of those churches which used Christianity to maintain national or ethnic identity. But let us not forget that it is possible to be equally uncatholic in other ways, as in maintaining a certain type of cultural Christianity so that it has the approval of a specific social class.

But, we may rightly ask, does catholicity mean an acceptance of any and every point of view? A readiness to believe everything and so end up believing nothing? Of course not. As we have already observed, the first use of the word *catholic* places Christ at the center; his openness is the norm of our acceptance of others. A catholicism which accepts and absorbs everything is not a true catholicism, because it amounts to a denial of the center to which everything else must harmonize. Catholicism is therefore not sheer breadth but an openness to accept all those whom Christ receives.

Richard McBrien, however, falls into a trap by ending his magnificent two-volume work *Catholicism* by claiming triumphalistically and uncharacteristically that "[Roman] Catholicism is character-ized by a *radical openness to all truth and to every value*. It is *comprehensive* and *all-embracing* toward the totality of Christian experience and tradition." He goes on to claim that there are no schools of theology which Catholicism excludes, no spiritualities which it denies, nor any doctrinal streams which it closes off.[5] I have the greatest respect for this writer, but the statement is just not true. The nature of Roman Catholicism is such that it does close off streams of spirituality and theologies which are incompatible with its own system of belief. The magisterium exists, in fact, to maintain the purity of Catholicism. As Walther von Loewenich observes, Roman Catholicism is not catholic enough to maintain the insights of Protestantism. "For all its universality, Roman Catholicism has never been broad enough to make room for simple, evangelical Christianity."[6]

To point this out is not to engage in unfriendly, polemical remarks, it is merely to underline the fact that true catholicity does not consist in holding incompatible truths in tension. It is not a giant umbrella under which all positions may shelter. But neither is it a narrow doctrinal orthodoxy which shelters only those who agree with *us*. If we are going to be committed to a genuinely open Christianity, we will be driven to maintain the breadth of the Christian tradition as we see it in Jesus, to be as open as he was to people, to be as accepting as he was of their sin and failure and blindness, to be as positive as he was in presenting the good news of the kingdom.

The second challenge which follows directly from this point is the uncomfortable fact that no church on this globe is truly catholic—not even the Roman Catholic Church—because the division of Christian-ity into different groups has meant that the whole church has lost its catholicity. As Zylstra comments, "How can a Christian confess one Lord of history when in the actual historical situation his followers pursue a hundred different directions?"[7] The situation drives Christians to pray for and to seek again that unity in love and doctrine which will draw us together under the banner of the one Lord. As Robert Webber points out, the two trends we should avoid as we seek a biblical catholicism are the spirit of sectarianism on the one hand

and the pat answer of "spiritual unity" on the other.[8] Catholics, indeed, are not the only ones in history who have regarded their own position as the right one; some Protestant groups have, from time to time, made exclusive claims for the wholeness of their interpretation of the faith and have as a result excluded many whom Christ would have included.

The very complexity of the problem may well daunt young Christians and make them wonder where on earth they will find this truly open community. The central element to keep in mind, however, is openness in Christ. We have to ask, Is this denomination open to other Christian bodies? Is it open to scriptural truth? Or is it characterized by a narrow, sectarian spirit?

A Holy Community

Another important mark of a faithful church is the attention it gives to being a holy people, a people set apart for God. In Christian history the holiness of the church has been treated in two major ways.

First, there has been a tendency to identify the holiness of the church with the holiness of its members. In the fourth and fifth centuries the Donatists of North Africa wanted to exclude from the church all those who had denied Christ in times of persecution. Even though these Christians wished to come back into fellowship, the Donatists took a rigorist line, arguing that a church which received such people back into its bosom ceased to be holy and thus ceased to be a church. The orthodox church answered that the church is like Noah's ark, containing both unclean and clean, or like the kingdom in Jesus' parable where the wheat and tares exist side by side until the final judgment. There have been many similar instances in church history when Christian groups have imposed a rigorous standard of holiness on others in order to maintain their notion of the purity of the body.

While we should reject an intolerant moral absolutism that imposes on people greater burdens than they can bear, we should also ask, Is there not, however, in this error a glimmer of truth which presents a challenge to the church today which has erred in the other direction?

We shall explore some aspects of this later.

The other tendency has been to absolutize the holiness of the church without regard for the sinfulness of its members. We have already observed that Catholics are particularly inclined to draw this distinction, idealizing the church and conceiving of it as having an existence independent of the sinful, fallible people which make it up. With this kind of reasoning it was always possible to keep at a distance the cries for church renewal and reform; because the church is holy, the problems stem from the people, never from the church and its structures.

While it is true that the church is greater than the sum of its members, it cannot exist apart from the people who give it its historical form. To accept and to acknowledge that the church is composed of sinful people is to confess that sinfulness and fallibility are part of the human condition and that they are also part of the structural reality of the church.

The weakness of the two approaches to understanding the church's holiness that we have considered is that in both the word *holy* has been reduced to a static idea which describes either the individual Christian or the church as possessing a moral perfection here and now. An alternative is to see that the church is holy, not in itself, but only in Christ and only in anticipation. The church that is holy is the one that will be presented to the Father by the Son as his bride without spot and wrinkle, because it will be presented as a purified community. On earth the church is human as well as divine, sinful as well as holy.

In the Bible, the term *holy* is invariably a dynamic, not a static, notion. It implies separation *for* God's service. Holy things and holy people are those objects and people set aside for God's use. They are not set aside for nothing, but for a definite and exclusive purpose. Israel was called to be a holy nation, separate from other nations in order to be God's instrument in the world (Ex 19:6). As Martin-Achard observes, "It is in so far as it is the Holy Nation, consecrated to its God, that it will reflect His Glory and testify to His holiness, and in this way, by its very existence in the world, it will assume its mediatorial function."[9]

The New Testament follows this Old Testament usage and links holiness to God's purposes for his people and the world. The term is both descriptive and prescriptive. It is *descriptive* because it speaks of a believer's relationship with his Lord. He is made holy in Christ. Christians in the New Testament are called saints, not because they are morally perfect and fit for heaven, but because they are accepted in Christ and share his holiness. The term is also *prescriptive* inasmuch as it points to the call of both the individual and the Christian community. Christians are sanctified in Christ, certainly, but they are also "called to be saints" (1 Cor 1:2; Rom 1:7). In the same way the church must maintain its holiness, remembering that its final destiny is to be the pure bride of Christ (Eph 5:27). The prescriptive force of holiness is eloquently set forth in the high priestly prayer of Jesus in John 17 where he prays that his disciples "may be sanctified in your truth" as a prelude to their mission. The consecration of the disciples to their task is parallel to Jesus' consecration to his own ministry. So he prayed, "For their sake I consecrate myself" (Jn 17:19), allowing no other purpose to compromise his mission.

As I see it then, the church's holiness is inextricably linked with its mission to represent Jesus Christ in the world. If this is the case, what does it have to say about the role of the church today? We shall consider two aspects which have a significant bearing on our theme.

The Message That the Church Proclaims. The church is a witnessing body called to declare the saving work of its master. By definition the church is that company of people consecrated to Jesus Christ and appointed by him to proclaim his love to the nations. Ecclesiology (the doctrine of the church) is therefore set firmly between the bounds of Christology (the doctrine of Christ) and soteriology (the doctrine of salvation). The church has no independent status of its own. It is an agent of the Lord and entrusted with a great message to pass on. The church dare not, like the wicked servant in Matthew's parable, hide its one precious talent in the ground. To depart from Jesus' message or to replace it with another is to depart from the Lord and to be an apostate people (Gal 1:6-9). The church, then, is committed to God's truth and under obligation not only to preserve it—the wicked servant did exactly that but got no credit for doing so—but to make it known. Paul, aware of the urgency of his task, cried, "Woe to me if I do not preach the gospel!" (1 Cor 9:16). The nettle must be grasped, therefore: doctrine matters. The holiness of the church affects the character of the message the church proclaims.

Yet the issue of doctrinal purity is far from simple, as nearly two thousand years of church history painfully show. But the march toward doctrinal agreement must continue. The church needs it for the sake of the world, because Christianity loses credibility as church groups compete for human hearts. Yet the church also needs doctrinal agreement for itself simply because mission and unity based on anything other than the essentials of the faith will not re-create the oneness which God desires for his people.

How are we to arrive at a common understanding on the message we proclaim? A rigid exclusivism is clearly not the way forward, because it allows no gray areas—everything must be black or white. On the other hand, the opposite extreme of tolerating any idea which looks even vaguely Christian is not the answer either.

These days there is an increasing cry for the recognition of theological pluralism. Proponents argue that unity will come only as we accept the legitimacy of different ways of contemplating divine truth. Carl Braaten, for example, writes that until a short while ago all churches could expect and even guarantee a broad consensus of doctrine within their ranks. But now, he contends, "every confessional group is penetrated by a multiplicity of beliefs on every basic doctrine."[10] Braaten gives two reasons for this. First, dialog with other Christians and other church groups has led to a new openness toward plurality of expression and understanding. Second, when churches enter into a dialog with the world, they open themselves to an infinite variety of new methods and new possibilities: "The church builds new doctrine by taking new cognitive materials from her surrounding culture into her theological life." The appraisal is basically true; such openness does lead to a deep enrichment of concepts previously unknown or frowned on. Even the monolithic character of the Roman Catholic system of belief has cracked as theological pluralism has entered the reality of its life.

What, then, does holiness mean for the church's sacred message? Is all theology good theology? Are there indeed no limits? Of course not. As Braaten goes on to point out, the Christian faith has a particular content. It makes a particular claim for the truth, that a particular man at a special point in time is Savior and Lord. "Any church that ceases to affirm this event and to live out its meaning has ceased to be a Christian community."[11]

And yet there is no final way of establishing the boundaries of doctrinal purity. The history of heresy shows that the church has usually had to react to heretical doctrine, not the other way around. The clarity of the New Testament did not stop heretical groups from forming doctrinal systems which denied explicit as well as implicit New Testament doctrine. The church's understanding of its faith was shaped gradually in opposition to those who wished to impose their own rigid interpretation on others. To some extent the formulation of doctrine which arises out of the clash with heresy always involves the appropriation of insights and understandings at the heart of the heresy, because no heresy is pure heresy. It always affirms as well as denies truth.

Today our task, hard as it is, must be to discuss with other Christians in love and respect the kind of pluralism which is truly biblical. Our task, in other words, is to steer a careful course between what we *must* affirm and what we are *compelled* to deny. We shall most probably find that different churches can affirm much together, especially about the person and work of Christ. But we must also be careful not to deny what the New Testament does not deny. The fullness of Christ's revelation must be our central reference point.

The World the Church Serves. "Be holy, for I am holy," said God to his people (Lev 11:44). The call to share God's moral perfection has sometimes been a temptation for the church to consider itself aloof from the world or even superior to it. In fact, one of the earliest errors was the notion that the world was created for the sake of the church. The idea of holiness that we have expounded is that the church is called not only to be separate from evil and to share the nature of God in a moral and spiritual sense, but also to reflect this in the world as a serving, caring and witnessing community.

There is, of course, nothing new in this idea, but the church has not always lived up to this goal. Indeed, we must acknowledge the difficulty in witnessing to God's values, on the one hand, and going into our society with a message of hope and reconciliation, on the other.

This twofold nature of consecration places the church in creative tension. In a helpful book written some years ago, Peter Berger explains what this means in sociological terms. The church, he says, in terms of its identity is what sociologists call a "cognitive minority," that is, a group whose world view contrasts sharply with that generally held by their contemporaries. A cognitive minority may react in either of two ways to the pressure of an alien world. They may retreat from their society into a ghetto where their belief structure is sheltered from the harsh, unfriendly winds which blow outside. Or, Berger observes, the minority group may "go native," surrendering itself to the established beliefs of the dominant culture.[12] The German theologian Jürgen Moltmann points similarly to the tension Christians experience between identity and relevance. The tighter and more self-conscious the identity of a Christian group, the further it distances itself from the world. In striving to retain its distinctiveness as a community, it sacrifices its relevance to culture. On the other hand, the more relevant it becomes by drawing closer to the world, the more it increases the risk of losing its identity and blurring the distinctiveness of the Christian message.[13]

These analyses of the church's situation help us make a conscious, Christian response to our society. We cannot afford to surrender ourselves to either of these alternatives alone. Consecration to Christ's truth places the people of God firmly between ghetto and cultural surrender. We must preserve our identity as a holy people, set apart for him.

Above all else, perhaps, Christians of mainstream Christianity need to recover a sense of morality and discipline. If the world is allowed to join the church on its own terms, the character of the church as a holy community will be lost completely. At the same time, the church is a missionary body, with truth to share with the outside world. If that truth is to be communicated effectively, the church has to adapt and use the cognitive and cultural tools that the outside world will understand. The now famous cry of Vatican II that the church is the "Light to the Nations" *(Lumen gentium)* sets out the biblical context of holiness. We are a pilgrim community on the march, using the insights and thought forms of our culture to convey the sacred message of Christ. We are in the world, but not of it.

The characterization of the church as holy, therefore, helps us to understand what it means for the church to be faithful to the gospel it has received. In *Mere Christianity,* C. S. Lewis makes holiness one of the touchstones of authentic Christianity. To the person contemplating church membership he asks the question, Is holiness there? The point he is making is that holiness will be glimpsed in the life, character and claims of the church of Jesus Christ. It should not be overrigorous in matters of discipline, yet it should maintain standards and identify with Christ's values. A holy church is recognizable.

A Unified Community

If we have found the use of such terms as *holy, catholic* and *apostolic* anachronistic when applied to the modern church, we shall find the description of the church as *one* even more so. It appears to be firmly negated by present facts. The World Council of Churches, consisting of over two hundred church bodies, is sufficient witness to the broken body of Christ. Alan Richardson remarks in his *Introduction to the Theology of the New Testament* that to speak of the World Council of Churches is an anomaly totally mysterious to the New Testament. It would be more correct, he observes, to speak of a World Council of Schisms and Heresies than of Churches, if precise New Testament meanings were given.[14]

We must, in all honesty, concede Alan Richardson's point. God is one; his Spirit is one; his message is one; his mission is one. But his people are divided. And how strikingly this contrasts with the unity of fellowship which pervades the New Testament! "Now the company of those who believed were of one heart and soul" (Acts 4:32).

This does not mean that there were no disagreements. There were. Squabbles arose over the care of Greek-speaking widows (Acts 6), about circumcision (Acts 15), over factions in church life (1 Cor 1). But when such difficulties arose, they were met and solutions found. No doubt the unity of the body was threatened in the first century, but the New Testament writers found it inconceivable that the people of God should separate into exclusive fellowships. Paul, dealing with the issue of party strife, asks incredulously, "Is Christ divided?" To him it is unthinkable that a church can be anything other than one. By the time the letter to the Ephesians was written the church was clearly viewed as worldwide (or catholic), united in a common faith in Christ. This unity of faith is firmly grounded on a confession of "one Lord, one faith, one baptism, one God and Father of us all" (Eph 4:5-6).

So much then for the unity of the New Testament church. But what is its challenge for us today? Two elements stand out as particular challenges.

A Spiritual Unity in Christ. While we must not undervalue the importance of membership in the visible church, we must recognize that membership in the body of Christ is constituted, not by the external marks of joining the church, but by spiritual birth. Catholic Christians may sigh at this point because it may seem to them the same incorrigible Protestant inclination to put faith before everything else. And it is true that the emphasis in the New Testament does not fall on our response but on God's grace. It is God's action that counts. As human beings we differ in many ways, but we are alike in that we cannot save ourselves. Salvation is a gift, and by accepting that gift we are made children of God and members of his family. The sacrament of baptism is indeed important, and for many Christians inseparable from the act of salvation itself, but such externals as the water, the words or the authority of the lawfully ordained minister or priest do not automatically save us. It is God's Spirit who gives us new birth, and that great event is not humanly determined. Paul argues this strongly in Romans. Having been justified by faith (5:1) and given the

Spirit as a seal (5:5), we receive the objective sign of this union in our baptism (6:3-4), which is a symbol of our death to the old life and our new birth.

This spiritual unity should dominate and color our whole theology of the church. Have as high a doctrine of the organic unity of the church as you like, so long as your doctrine of spiritual birth is higher. We are all one in Christ Jesus. We cannot classify Christians by human organizations; we dare not say definitely that all Catholics are Christians or that all Baptists or all Methodists are Christians, or that unbaptized people cannot be Christians. Our ecclesiastical rules cannot confine God's Spirit—the Spirit leaps over human barriers.

Moltmann arrives at a similar conclusion and links unity with the centrality of the cross: "Ecumenism comes into being wherever—and this is everywhere—we find ourselves under the cross of Christ and there recognize each other as brothers and sisters who are hungry in the same poverty and imprisoned in the selfsame sin. Under the cross we all stand empty-handed. We have nothing to offer except the burden of our guilt and the emptiness of our hearts. We do not stand under the cross as Protestants, as Catholics, or as adherents to Orthodoxy. . . . The nearer we come to Christ's cross, the nearer we come together."[15]

The fact of spiritual unity throws into relief the total absurdity of all claims which dechurch others. Do we really think that God has favorites and directs his grace accordingly? Surely in his mind there is no such thing as the Catholic Church, Anglican Church, Methodist, Baptist and so on. Hans Küng urges us, in fact, to see the church from God's angle, to see it as his cherished and pure bride, although from our perspective it is sinful and divided.[16]

Such an emphasis on spiritual unity encourages us to affirm all those who confess Christ. If we have nothing to offer God as far as our salvation is concerned, we have no grounds for boasting about our church membership. If we are not one with him spiritually, our church affiliation is of no consequence whatever.

Confessional Unity. The spiritual unity of all Christians is primary, as we have seen, but it does not give us warrant to be casual about our membership in the visible family of God. We dare not fold our arms complacently, assuming that spiritual unity is all that matters to God. Indeed not. So long as Christendom is divided we live in a world where Christians who confess the same Lord are unreconciled to one another. Theologically this is a scandal, because in Christ, Paul tells us, "there is neither Jew nor Greek, slave nor free, male nor female, for you are all one in Christ Jesus" (Gal 3:28 NIV). How empty that cry would have been if Paul were writing today! But also from the viewpoint of the church's mission, as we have already noted, the disunity of Christianity constitutes a major stumbling block to the progress of the faith. On what basis is it possible for the church, entrusted with such a marvelous message of reconciliation, to go to a divided world when it needs reconciliation within?

However, we need not despair of a church which seems to fall short of God's ideal. Unity is worth struggling for because the church has a fundamental responsibility to be the sign of God's kingdom. There are two aspects of this struggle we ought to keep before us.

First, our hope is that in mission we might recover our visible unity.[17] If the heart of the gospel is that "God was in Christ reconciling the world to himself," and if he has committed to his people the word of reconciliation, then it is a matter of top priority for the church to declare these truths in its life. In other words, mission forces the church to be one, and that oneness will make her a more effective agent of the kingdom. Indeed, we know from experience that churches which engage in service and outreach find themselves drawn together toward a previously undiscovered bond and unity.

Second, if we have not already done so, we have to make choices about church membership. But, sadly and ironically, as we do we perpetuate the divisions of Christianity. We do this innocently, of course, but we cannot be a Baptist, a Methodist, a Catholic, without deciding against something else, and so the legacy of the past sentences us to exclude others and be excluded. This is something we cannot alter. But we do have the freedom to do something with the present. Is it our desire, then, to seek the unity of God's people? Have we a passion to see the church made whole and reunited in Christ? Do we long for the church to be a shining example of how people should live and honor one another? If we echo these sentiments, then each of us can act as an agent of God to make this unity a fact.

One thing we must remind ourselves. Unity is not uniformity. The existence of separate Christian groups in one area is not in itself incompatible with unity, any more than the house churches of the New Testament represented a division of the total Christian body in one place. Many of our denominational churches reflect different temperamental or sociological leanings and so enrich the body of Christ by the variety they express. A dull uniformity is not the quest of unity. Rather, what divides Christianity is the refusal to accept one another in Christ, and this is tragically mirrored in denominational bans which forbid our meeting around the table of the Lord. The table of unity thus becomes the center of disunity, and Christ is divided again. Christians cannot be content with this.

I Believe in One Holy Catholic and Apostolic Church

"I believe in one holy catholic and apostolic church," remarked Archbishop William Temple, "but regret that it doesn't exist."

We might well share this opinion after our analysis of these four marks of the church. The disunity and the sinfulness of the Christian groups which call themselves the body of Christ mock our grandiose claims. The gulf between the eschatological vision of a perfectly holy, worldwide, united church of God, anchored firmly in the apostles' teaching and life, and that of the earthly reality of a torn and bedraggled church could not be wider.

This is our present situation. We must now apply some of these insights to help young Christians answer such questions as, How do I recognize a true Christian fellowship? What are the marks of an authentic church? Should I be in fellowship with that congregation or this one?

If we are already members of a mainline denominational church, we should not be tempted to leave it unless there are compelling reasons. Central to these should be doctrinal reasons. We have already stressed the sinfulness of division, and to leave a faithful Christian communion and go elsewhere is sin. God hates the sin of division. Our allegiance to the church is part of our commitment to the gospel of Jesus. His call to us to join him is also a call to join his people. Protestant Christians are more guilty than others of allowing secondary matters to affect their church affiliation. All kinds of things, some of them trivial to the extreme, have led us to change our membership—the personality of the minister, the character of the preaching, the type of music, the social life of the church, the type of service used, the financial standing of the church, the numbers attending it and so on.

Somehow we must differentiate between the *essential* marks of a church, which make an authentic, living Christian presence, and *desirable* qualities which we might personally feel would make it a more orderly and vigorous church of God.[18] And we must make sure that the difference between essential and desirable is carefully preserved; otherwise we fall into the old trap of creating barriers which exclude other Christians.

Richard McBrien, for example, asks the question, "Why should one be a Catholic rather than a Protestant or an Orthodox?" He responds by saying that it is allegiance to the papacy which distinguishes Catholicism. "The source of unity is the Eucharist, and the ministerial or hierarchical foundation of the Eucharist is the College of Bishops with the Pope at the centre and the head."[19] McBrien does not want to make this essential for all Christians, because he later affirms that Catholics and Protestants agree in the essentials of the faith: "Both confess Jesus is Lord, share a common baptism, have a reverence for Scripture and a love for the gospel." Other Christian denominations might want to put the emphasis elsewhere by delineating what they particularly require of their members. Now this is quite all right. Each denomination has a right to impose its own church order on its worshipers, but we must not confuse church order with the essential marks which separate the true body of Christ from the false one.

We must remind ourselves again that we are talking about a visible congregation. We cannot say of any congregation that they are a definite group of born-again believers. We can never know that. All we know is that they profess the Christian faith. We do not know the depth, extent or integrity of anyone's faith; as we observed earlier, every congregation is composed of men and women at every stage of Christian development. What unites the visible body is not a spiritual unity in Christ but a professed faith in him. And here we approach an essential mark of a Christian community: it is a fellowship united in the conviction that Jesus is Lord and Savior. This is New Testament faith, and it will distinguish an authentic church from a false one. No matter what claims a church makes concerning its antiquity or success, if it has a low view of Christ or if his revelation is not considered to be final or complete, it will be a congregation to avoid. A church of Jesus Christ will proclaim his full deity with its consequent Trinitarian development that this Jesus is part of the Godhead comprising Father, Son and Holy Spirit, and that this Jesus is the only Savior and the only mediator between God and man. The community based on this foundation will want to emphasize the sufficiency of his grace and the provision of his resources for all Christians.

A second essential mark of a genuine Christian fellowship is that it is anchored in Scripture and seeks to be faithful to its witness and renewed by its life. W. A. Visser 't Hooft, former general secretary of the World Council of Churches, points out that "a church in whom the Bible will have the last word will never be able to forget that it is not the kingdom of God and that it lives under the constant judgment of God."[20] Why is it important, however, for the Bible to have the last word, to use Visser 't Hooft's phrase? Because the Bible is the authentic witness and record of the radical new event of Christ. The new covenant makes the biblical testimony absolutely crucial. Every genuine Christian experience and event flows from this primary Christ event, but we can only tell that an experience is true by its conformity to scriptural teaching. Some subnormal Christian sects have slipped into error either by adding to scriptural revelation, such as the Mormons, or by reducing it to fit a prescribed philosophy, such as Jehovah's Witnesses.

To acknowledge the centrality of Scripture entails a willingness to be changed and renewed. A biblical church will not be static, stuck

in the past and voicing shibboleths from a bygone era. It will be open
to new things and willing to adapt to new circumstances. It is
heartening to see that there is increasing acceptance of this from
Catholics as well as Protestants. Yves Congar comments, "We can
freely admit that if reunion does take place one day, it will be with
a Church which differs in some way from the present condition of the
Catholic Church, different because it will have developed and been
purified and refined in more than one respect through its deepest
sources, particularly with Holy Scripture."[21]

We must not think complacently that this is only a word for
Catholics. Indeed not. For even a sound theological system may
prevent us from receiving the Word directly if our attention is on
keeping to its rules and not the teaching of the Bible. John Van Dyk
comments on the inability of Protestant churches to meet in unity and
sees the problem in their failure to really be *under* the Word. "To say:
'We stand on the Bible, sola scriptura' simply will not do. Ever since
the Reformation, Protestantism has said: 'Sola scriptura!'—and look
what has happened."[22] How true that is and how sadly ironical that
so-called Bible churches have sometimes separated from each other on
minor theological issues. All churches and congregations must hear
the Word afresh and not come to it expecting it to repeat our already
formulated views.

A third essential I look for in a church is the primacy of the
sacraments. Others may possibly want to see the sacraments as
desirable but not essential, because there are sound Christian
fellowships, such as the Salvation Army, which do not observe the
sacraments. I certainly have no desire to exclude the Salvation Army,
whom I see as within the body of Christ. However, I consider them
to be an exceptional case. As the sacraments of baptism and the Lord's
Supper have been historic, visible signs of the gospel, I believe that
it is right to see them faithfully expressed in the life of the church.
There is, after all, an unambiguous witness to them in the New
Testament. Jesus submitted to baptism, and, following his resurrection, he commanded his disciples to baptize in his name. Although
Paul put the preaching of the gospel before baptizing people (1 Cor

1:17), his reference to the theology of baptism shows its importance in the life of the early church (Col 2:12; Rom 6). The same applies to Holy Communion. Jesus called on his followers to repeat his last meal, and the apostolic church obeyed this faithfully (1 Cor 11:23).

I stand by these three aspects as essential marks of a true Christian community. Others may want to put the emphasis elsewhere, by holding, for example, that official office-bearers of the church must be instituted in a certain way, that a certain baptismal policy must prevail or that a certain type of service is essential. I would not want, however, to describe such requirements as essential to the Christian faith, because their authority does not come from the Lord but from the later church. There may be good reasons for the sake of church order for embracing monoepiscopacy, for example, but I find no cogent reason for saying that it is of the essence of Christianity. I might well consider it desirable as a form of church order, and it may be an element that would lead me to choose this Christian community rather than that one, but to make monoepiscopacy binding on all Christians as a dogma to accept would be to place on them a burden the New Testament does not make.

Whatever church we join, we must remember that we are not doing God a favor. We are compelled by reason of our baptism to belong to his people. Once we have prayerfully accepted membership in a local church, our duty is to support, help and encourage that fellowship, using such talents as God has given to us to contribute to its life. And it is to be hoped that as we settle into that fellowship we will help to make it more open to other churches, helping it to lovingly affirm all other churches where Christ is preached and where people try to walk according to his standards.

Chapter 8
HARBOR
IN SIGHT?

*F*rom time to time I am asked how I see the future of relationships between Catholics and Protestants. Is unity possible in this century? Crystal-ball gazing has never been one of my specialities, and I have always found this a difficult question to answer. From one point of view, I could give a confident yes; yes, if we really desired unity, if we really loved one another, if young and old decided to refuse to allow history to dictate policy to us. "Where there's a will there's a way" is an aggressive business philosophy, but it applies to Christian unity as well.

On the other hand, the will to embrace one another in unity is lacking in both traditions. The majority of Christians are not convinced that the unity of the church is essential. While we pay lip service to the call for unity, our hearts do not beat in time with this desire so precious to Jesus. We must add to this another fact, that the pathway to unity is barred in both traditions by minority groups who will not budge from well-established, well-entrenched positions. Unity *on our terms* is the unspoken attitude, and this, of course, makes it difficult for churches to make strides forward.

Realism about the present situation therefore dictates, and I have to reply, "It is true that dialog and cooperation are increasing all the time, but unity before the end of this century is unlikely for two reasons. The majority of Christians are apathetic about it, and a strong minority are militantly opposed to it."

And that is really a sobering thing to say even though facts are on my side. Sobering, because it goes directly against God's will for his people. The gospel, after all, is about reconciliation—unity between God and man, and unity among his people. It was Christ's intention to bring all people together through his cross, "to reconcile to himself all things, . . . making peace by the blood of his cross" (Col 1:20). This, Paul declared, was God's program which began with Christ's death on the cross.

Unity, indeed, is one of the great New Testament themes, and Paul returns to it in Ephesians 2 where he speaks of Christ making peace, reconciling us to God. Now if this, in brief, is the effect of the gospel on the church, we must see disunity as one of the most terrible diseases of the body. Let us see disunity as it really is—the ugly blasphemy which mocks the cross of Christ and insults his name. Yet, in truth, it is even more than that because our disunity confounds the gospel of unity that we preach.

Yet even though I am concerned by the apathy and lack of love shown by Christians who should know better, the ferment in the churches created by the Holy Spirit is such an exciting phenomenon that I am never without hope. Indeed, as we have already observed, we are living at a time when God is doing new things, renewing his people and reviving his work. God is bringing his children together. We are beginning to see that against the world's urgent problems— the indifference of secularism, the militancy of Communism and other ideologies, the lostness of humankind, the vast problems confronting the nations—Christians have more that unites them than what divides them. We have begun to move toward one another. The signs include:
□ *theological dialog* no longer based on polemics but on a desire to understand and heal the past, characterized by a number of interfaith Conversations that are still going on,

☐ *worship* as Christians from different traditions worship and pray together,

☐ *charismatic experience* as mainstream denominations have been penetrated by the renewal movement, leading to fresh insight from the Spirit and vital Christian experience,

☐ *the personal challenge* individual Christians have experienced to consider the contributions each of us can make to the cause of Christian unity.

That is why, in spite of the enormous odds to be overcome, I am a man of hope. But how can we make hope a reality? There are a number of practical ways we may accelerate the progress of unity and bring the harbor into view.

Accepting One Another

When I accept another Christian as a Christian brother or sister, I assume that in spite of the differences between us we still belong to one family, the Christian church. Later we shall consider the theological basis which makes that a possibility, but for the moment we must consider the ingrained assumptions that still bar the way to accepting one another.

First is an assumption that even if we use the word *church* freely of one another's denomination, some are more *church* than others. This is a little like the attitude of the pigs in Orwell's *Animal Farm*. The pigs, who are the elite of the community, justify their position by saying, "All are equal, but some are more equal than others." My own denomination, sadly, has had this attitude toward non-Catholic churches in Britain. Because they do not share our episcopal form of ministry and ordination, we refuse to allow them to place their ministry on a plane with ours. While we are extremely polite and often apparently humble about this, the theology on which this is erected— namely, that episcopal ordination conveys the special grace of Christ which goes back through the bishops of the church to Peter himself— is highly suspect.

And what we do on a small scale, the Church of Rome does on a larger scale to the rest of Christendom. Anglican arrogance is eclipsed by Rome's, but it is the same mistake. We may be proud of our form of church government, but we ought not to assume that God's grace is absent one whit from other forms. We must accept the ministries of other churches and allow that acceptance to work out to all Christians. And, what is more, we should show our acceptance by inviting other ministers to take part in our services, even taking those cherished symbolic parts that we hold dear and that are central to our divisions.

Then, second, there are ingrained assumptions against minority congregations. On the continent, Catholicism holds sway, and all else is insignificant by comparison. In Britain, the Anglican Church is the established church, while in the States churches like the Baptists and Methodists as well as the Roman Catholics have large fellowships. Without realizing it, such churches may use their power to restrict the freedom of others by refusing to accept the church life of other traditions. A strong church may find itself thinking, "We are comfortably off, why should we change? What can we learn from others? What can these people give us?" And yet Christ taught us to serve one another, to wash the feet of other disciples and not to choose the most important seat in the synagogue. Should not Christ's attitude be our own? What the New Testament clearly shows is that Christ was the great reconciler who came to do something about relationships, not only between God and man, but also between estranged social groups. He mixed freely with all kinds of people and became the center of reconciliation. Disciples of Jesus ought to do the same.

Talking and Worshiping Together

Part of accepting one another should include talking to one another and worshiping together. In my final year in Durham, I was chairman of the Durham Council of Churches, and during the Week of Prayer for Christian Unity we tried an experiment. We invited local congregations to come together for a supper with a view to discussing certain questions set by Lord Ramsey, who had preached the night before. I was struck by the way that the ordinary act of eating drew us all together.

People arrived in their denominational groups, and as they entered the church they huddled together in those groups—Catholics, Anglicans, Baptists and so on. Then we began to eat and to chat over the buffet meal. Following this we split into discussion groups. By the end of the evening, we had grown considerably in our understanding of one another—in the way we approached the Christian faith, in the way we perceived one another and, most important, in our common understanding of Christ as Lord. That supper made a considerable contribution to cross-denominational relationships in Durham, and yet it was simple. All we did was meet for a meal and talk together.

Talking in any context is preliminary to healing and reconciliation. Study any political and social difficulty and we see that as long as representatives are talking there is hope. "Talks are going on between the Government and the Railway Unions" says that the bargaining may be hard but possibilities for solving the problems still exist. But when we read that "talks have broken down," the sides are further apart than ever. Somehow the talking must start before reunion can take place. And this is surely true for Christians too. It is good to hear of theological Conversations going on between Catholic and Protestant theologians, but they are only part of the conversations that ought to be taking place. Unless ordinary Christians are meeting and talking as well, the theological talks are apt to be irrelevant to the grass roots of the church. Both kinds of conversations are necessary for such long-divided communions to draw together.

Part of this talking includes talking to God together in worship. The word *worship* derives from the Old English *worthship*, that is, we give God the honor and praise due him. True worship flows not from beautiful liturgy, fine prayers, majestic singing—important as these may be—but from a meeting between God and his people which centers on Jesus Christ. Humility is the primary precondition of worship. When we enter God's presence—whether it be in a cathedral, mission hall or among a small group of friends in a room—effective worship does not depend on the place or the liturgy, but whether we belong to God or not.

How simple this is, and how difficult we make worship seem! This

is where charismatic renewal has made its most significant contribution, I believe. There have been many revivals in history, but none, as
far as I know, have ever brought such apparently different Christian
groups as Catholics and evangelicals together. Charismatic renewal
has, and it has achieved this based on our unity in Jesus and focusing
on worship which flows from that central point. In so doing, the
renewal movement has taken our differences in worship as being as
important as our similarities. Instead of pretending that they do not
exist, this movement of the Spirit has emphasized that the differences
are due not only to cultural and emotional factors but also to the work
of the Spirit, who does not want us to be the same.

The English Christian singer Ishmael describes worship in these
words:

Lord, we come to worship,
Lord, we come to praise,
Lord, we come to worship you in,
Oh, so many ways.
Some of us shout,
Some of us sing,
Some of us whisper the praise we bring,
But, Lord, we all are gathering
To bring to you our praise.

The differences Ishmael describes are certainly relevant to our unity
with other Christians. Uniformity is not the goal. Unity in worship
doesn't mean that. True unity accepts different forms of expression
even if some individual expressions are not common to all.

But what are the implications of this for worshiping together and
especially for sharing in the Lord's Supper? In an important book on
the church, Jürgen Moltmann has argued against restricting Holy
Communion to "our" people. Arrive at unity first, it is often argued,
and then we can meet around the table of the Lord, the symbol of
unity. Moltmann responds that it is precisely because it is the Lord's
table that we have no right to fence it in. Catholics fence Episcopalians
out, Episcopalians fence Nonconformists out, gospel halls sometimes
fence out those who do not belong, and so on. We have made it *our*

table but we call it the Lord's.[1]

Whether the following action was influenced by Moltmann I cannot say, but a few years ago former Archbishop of Canterbury Donald Coggan made his famous appeal for intercommunion. "While we are searching for our unity," he argued, "let us meet together for Holy Communion. Let us not debar one another from fellowship around the sacrament of unity." His appeal fell on deaf ears. Theologians on both sides considered that this advice would lead to a reckless ignoring of real differences between Catholic and Protestant Christians. But I suspect that Christian insight and compassion are on his side. How many of us, I wonder, have found ourselves in situations in which the rules of our churches contradict our consciences or instinct?

This poses for many Christians a real moral dilemma. If the rule at their church is that Holy Communion at another denominational fellowship is forbidden or discouraged, do they obey this rule as loyal members of their church? Or do they disobey it because they feel that in this instance the church's ruling is wrong?

Toward a Hierarchy of Truths
In our personal lives, we recognize that we cannot undo the past. We may deeply regret some events in our lives, but we can do nothing about them. They are gone, even though their impact remains with us to this day. That, in fact, is the important thing about history, whether we are talking about our own or that of the world in general. History shapes us and makes us richer or poorer according to its legacy. It is not simply back there, but it enters our present. It is a little like a social genetic code which imprints its character on our lives.

Nowhere is this more true than in the historical and cultural heritage we call the Christian faith. Underneath that general umbrella we have separated into our cozy denominational lives fed by our divergent traditions. We have been taught to treasure our faith, to treat it as more authentic than other traditions, to regard it as *The Truth* untainted with error. This is where the yearning for unity, felt by so many of us, is held back; the issues extend deeply into our separate histories. How can Protestants with their faith anchored in the New Testament have unity with Catholics, whose official teachings include doctrines they cannot accept? The question is reciprocated from the Catholic side. How can the historical faith of the church be reconciled with the somewhat reduced faith of the Protestants? Good will is clearly not enough. We have not got a good-natured, ecclesiastical fairy godmother who can wave history away with a flourish of her magic wand. We are stuck with our opposing views. Or are we?

There is, I believe, a way through this dilemma. The Second Vatican Council, in fact, opened new possibilities through a statement in the Decree on Ecumenism. The decree suggested that closer agreement among Christians is possible if we think in terms of a hierarchy of truths. What the decree is getting at is this: unity is often barred by the attention given to our differences, but not all doctrines have the same importance for faith. Could we arrive at an understanding of the common core of the faith we share while allowing freedom with respect to other teachings less essential?

This looks like a promising way forward. It is biblically true that not all the doctrines of the Christian faith have the same value for *saving faith* even if they are regarded as important in their own right. Take the doctrine of the Virgin Mary. Clearly our understanding of Mary is not as central to the Christian faith as our understanding of the resurrection. Likewise, the doctrine of the church as one holy catholic and apostolic body does not have the same implications for faith as the doctrine of the Trinity. And we could go on to name many other elements of New Testament Christianity which, although part of our inheritance in the faith, have never been deemed essential for public confessions of faith in Christ. Indeed, the earliest baptismal confession, "Jesus is Lord," and the Christian credo of the catacombs, "Jesus Christ, God's Son, Savior," seem bare in comparison with later creeds. Yet they were seen by the early Christians as conveying all that was necessary to identify the faithful.

Of course, I can appreciate that many Catholics might not like the idea of some dogmas like papal infallibility and the Marian dogmas being considered dispensable by some sections of the church. Surely, they will say, if it is regarded as part of the essence of Catholicism to believe in infallibility, can we make this a dispensable garment, saying to other Christians, "Do try this on for size. If you find it too uncomfortable, you don't have to wear it." They might add that there is a wholeness about the Catholic faith, not detachable bits which can be separated from a center. However, Protestants could perhaps meet the unease of Catholic friends by pointing out that for nineteen hundred years the Christian churches got along quite happily without the formulated dogmas of infallibility, the Immaculate Conception or the bodily Assumption of Mary into heaven. Even if some might contend that these doctrines were held implicitly by the church before they were officially promulgated, they were not required as articles of belief. So, perhaps defining a hierarchy of beliefs will enable us to establish a common core of truths around which we can affirm our Christian identity.

As this is obviously important for the unity of the church today, let's push it a little further. How do I recognize the faith of another? We tackled this issue in part in the last chapter, but it is now time to answer the question more definitively.

My own view is that the Christian who wants to be true to the Bible and to historic Christianity will wish to cling to the following six central points enshrined in the ancient creed of the church.

1. That Jesus Christ is Lord and Savior. The New Testament is emphatic about this. The life and deeds of Jesus are definitive. We can speak of him, testify to him and represent him, but we can never add anything new to his work. He is unique and incomparable. He is Christianity's cornerstone or, in the eyes of the world, its stumbling block. The cardinal importance of the Lord is underlined by the fact that the heresies and squabbles of the first five centuries centered mainly on the person of Christ; the church had to resist the pressure to move him from its heart.

2. That the nature of God is Trinitarian. God has revealed himself visibly in Jesus and powerfully through the Spirit. Christians embrace a Trinitarian faith in which God is experienced as Creator, Savior and

Sanctifier. We dare not slide away into a theism which makes God the Father an aloof, uncomprehending deity, or the Son a benign man from Galilee, or the Spirit merely an influence of God. The Trinity is the formulation of the outworking of the ministry of God in our world. Indeed, the testimony of Christians down the centuries is that they have experienced God as Creator, Savior and Sanctifier.

3. *That faith in Jesus and baptism into him through the Trinitarian confession constitute the new birth and the initiatory rite into the church.* The believer is made a child of God and a member of Christ's universal church. Through baptism we enter into God's family.

4. *That through the Holy Spirit the Christian church is constituted and that it takes all ministries and gifts in the body to express the fullness of the catholic faith.* The church is brought into existence by two commands of Christ. The first constitutes it as a worshiping body: "Do this in remembrance of me." As the church obeys that command and meets around the table of the Lord, where he is the host and we his guests, we are built up to be a body for his glory. The second command constitutes the church as a witnessing and serving body: "Go into all the world and preach the gospel." As a missionary body the church exists for the benefit of others and grows in faithfully caring for others and proclaiming Christ to them.

5. *That our faith is divinely revealed in Scripture and expressed in the ancient creeds of the church.* All Christian teaching must be rooted in Scripture and consistent with it. Tradition will, indeed, have its proper place in the life of God's people. The church of God is a historical community, and the riches of the faith, as well as the experience of God's love and power, are handed on from generation to generation. But church teaching, however venerable its history, must conform to the testimony of Scripture. Tradition has no independent status of its own.

6. *That Jesus Christ will come again in glory as Lord, Judge and Savior.* History awaits its fulfillment in him. His kingdom is coming.

Now, a basis of belief along these lines has much to commend it because it is recognizably orthodox and scriptural, yet not too tight to exclude justifiable variations. If there is a common heart to our faith, we can allow theological variations out of respect for the insights of different traditions. I recognize that the Virgin Mary has a deep and personal place in the devotional lives of many Christians. I respect that Marian strand in Christian tradition and would say that as long as it does not obscure Christ's pre-eminent role, we who are Protestants can accept that Catholic emphasis and try to learn from it. Similarly, the many other differences noted in the previous chapters may still have useful roles in the spiritual lives of Catholics and Protestants as long as the central thrust of the faith is not displaced.

Living the Life of the Spirit

Pentecost is commonly called the "birthday of the church" because on that day the Spirit fell with power on the assembled disciples and transformed them into a united missionary body. But Pentecost, besides representing the start of something, also symmbolized the completion of Christ's work, filling the followers of Jesus with his Spirit and giving them his joy and power. Lucien Cerfaux says aptly: "The Holy Spirit perfects Christians. Those first disciples in Jerusalem had lived with Christ, and they remained 'imperfect,' 'unfinished' until the day of Pentecost. It was not until then that they received their supreme consecration, but till then they had been clumsily trying to copy their master; the Spirit on the day of Pentecost finished the painting. Every now and again, we are told, Rubens would seize the brush from the hand of a pupil and over hesitant lines there would pass a breath of life."[2]

This new life in the Spirit, which all Christians share, has many implications for our agenda for change. First, it encourages us to appreciate what the Spirit is doing in the lives of all Christians and all denominations. The spirit of the world frequently tempts us to judge other believers, to write them off or to consider them to be second-class Christians. But if our concept of the Spirit is that his fresh life is available to all followers of Jesus, we may have to revise our opinion and see other believers as brothers and sisters in the same faith.

Second, as we might expect, the Holy Spirit never keeps still; he is always on the move creating new things or bringing life out of death. Among the many exciting things he is doing, the charismatic movement has a special place because not only has it introduced new life into the body, but it has also ushered in a great sense of freedom and openness. Although not all Christians may want to lay claim to being charismatic, the word *charismatic* is useful as a label in describing a person's attitude to the Spirit in the church. I see it as saying, "All that the New Testament claims for Christian experience we claim too; we want to share in the gifts and fruits of the Spirit." Although in some charismatic circles great emphasis is placed on receiving the Spirit and especially the gift of tongues as indicating baptism in the Spirit, I think that this is unimportant alongside the desire to be open to anything that the Spirit might want to give us or make of us in Jesus. We have already noted that charismatic renewal is exciting ecumenically because it has created a context in which Christians of all denominations meet for worship and service. It has had, and is having, an important ministry breaking down ecclesiastical barriers and revealing areas of deep unity which unite all those who love Christ.

And then I must add, finally, that life in the Spirit leads to change. Curiously enough, in a number of passages Paul contrasts the Holy Spirit with a spirit of fear. "You did not receive a spirit that makes you a slave again to fear, but you received the Spirit of sonship. And by him we cry, 'Abba, Father' " (Rom 8:15 NIV). The point Paul is making is that in Christ a new relationship of sonship exists from which fear is excluded. The Christian has moved from slavery to freedom. Fear is a factor that frequently bedevils unity talks, although it is usually undisclosed. We are afraid of losing our identity, our status, our traditions, our treasured liturgies and so on. The result is that the fear of change, of what might happen, makes us look back to what we have got, and so we cling to it more tenaciously than ever. The Spirit, however, looks ahead to the future; he wants us to travel on to unknown possibilities. In order to obtain what he has in store for us, we have to let go.

This is as true in the individual Christian life as it is in the church itself. We cannot become Christians or enjoy all that God promises unless we are prepared to turn our backs on what has gone before. The same truth holds on the larger scale: there cannot be true unity unless we are willing to sacrifice the things we hold dear to gain that which pleases God and unites his people.

Become Initiators of Change

As I write this final section, I have young Christians in mind, although I would like to think that what I have to say applies to all Christians who are open to new possibilities. But my comments apply particularly to younger people because they will have more opportunity than older Christians to bring change about.

It has become evident from our study that churches are saddled with luggage that comes to them from the heritage of the past. Sadly, this has resulted in hesitation, indecision and fear. Little wonder young Christians get impatient and disillusioned by the churches' slowness! "Surely," they say, "if we are all one in Christ Jesus, can't we make faster progress than this?"

I am sure we can. But effective change is related to three aspects of the Christian life which we all need to take seriously. First, those who wish to be initiators of change must be people of *prayer*. "Prayer changes things," goes the old chorus. And as our prayers for a united, witnessing church become more urgent and central, the reality will draw nearer. It's strange how we think of prayer as an inactive thing. But as the history of revivals and renewals shows, prayer is crucial. A praying church is always a living, adapting body. Christians who love the Lord of the church and pray for the renewal of his church will be in the forefront of change.

In addition, we must be people of *truth*. This book has tried not to duck important issues. No doubt readers are able to tell what I hold dear in my faith. In our dialog with one another we are not asked to surrender everything but rather to speak the truth as we see it in Jesus Christ. Truth and the essentials of the faith would suffer if dialog among the denominations ended up as a mishmash of uncertainties and vague beliefs. Hard questions must be put to one another, but how they are put will greatly affect the outcome. If history has taught us anything, we will not retreat into polemics. Beware of the polemical preacher; he is half-blind to truth because he fails to see that love must be part of the truth of Christ. Followers of Christ will always do their talking in the light of the death and resurrection of Jesus. Where he is central, not much divides.

Finally, I would like to see more of the *revolutionizing Spirit* in the lives of Christians everywhere. Let's have a little more divine dissatisfaction with the disunity of Christianity, and let's work for revolution. I remember the second National Evangelical Congress at Nottingham in 1979. At the debate on Catholicism, a Roman Catholic observer stood up and thanked evangelicals for their views. He then made this appeal: "Please don't hide behind your faith. Go home from this Congress and make friends with Catholic Christians. You may be surprised how much you have in common." I don't know how many followed his advice, but I do wish that Christians will feel increasingly able to climb out of their bomb shelters and cross that no man's land of fear and suspicion, not to engage in hand-to-hand combat, but to end this civil war which has weakened historic Christianity and which mocks the name of Christ.

"If all churches and communities really grow in the fullness of the Lord," said Pope John Paul II in 1980 when he addressed Protestant and Catholic Christians in Germany, "his Spirit will certainly indicate for us the way to reach full internal and external unity of the church." Amen to that!

Notes

Chapter 1: The Renewing Stream

[1]The sixteen official texts of the Second Vatican Council are published in *The Documents of Vatican II*, ed. Walter M. Abbott, S. J. (London: Geoffrey Chapman, 1966).

[2]See William McSweeney, *Roman Catholicism: The Search for Relevance* (New York: St. Martin's; Oxford: Blackwell, 1980), chapter five.

[3]Walther von Loewenich, *Modern Catholicism* (New York: St. Martin's; London: Macmillan, 1959), pp. 133-34.

[4]*Dei verbum* 1.2.

[5]*Dei verbum* 6.21.

[6]See *Dei verbum* 2.9-10.

[7]*Dei verbum* 6.21-22.

[8]Abbott, *Documents of Vatican II*, p. 339.

[9]Quoted by Abbott, *Documents of Vatican II*, p. 338.

[10]*Decree on Ecumenism* 2.7.

[11]*Decree on Ecumenism* 2.8.

[12]McSweeney, *Roman Catholicism*, p. 162. See also Gerard Noel, *The Anatomy of the Catholic Church* (Garden City, N.Y.: Doubleday; London: Hodder & Stoughton, 1980), chapter five.

[13]Lesslie Newbigin, *The Reunion of the Church* (London: SCM, 1948). A reprint edition, copyright 1960, was issued in 1979 by Greenwood Press, Westport, Conn.

[14]See Hendrik Kraemer, *A Theology of the Laity* (Philadelphia: Westminster; Guildford: Lutterworth, 1958).

Chapter 2: Troubled Waters

[1]For a short and readable account of Reformation issues, see James Atkinson, *Rome and Reformation* (London: Hodder & Stoughton, 1966). Also see Hans Küng, *The Council and Reunion* (New York and London: Sheed & Ward, 1961), chapter four.

[2]The literature on justification is vast, but see particularly J. A. Ziesler, *The Meaning of Righteousness in Paul* (Cambridge: Cambridge Univ. Press,

1972) and *The Great Acquittal,* ed. Gavin Reid (London: Collins, 1980).
[3]See Richard P. McBrien, *Catholicism* (Minneapolis: Winston; London: Geoffrey Chapman, 1980), pp. 308-10.

Chapter 3: Currents of Faith

[1]The theological issues are outlined clearly in von Loewenich, *Modern Catholicism,* chapter seven.

[2]Hans Küng, *Justification: The Doctrine of Karl Barth and a Catholic Reflection* (New York: Nelson; London: Burns and Oates, 1964).

[3]For a more developed analysis of Küng's arguments, see my article in *The Great Acquittal.*

[4]So, Louis Bouyer, *The Spirit and Forms of Protestantism* (Westminster, Md.: Newman; London: The Harvil Press, 1955). Bouyer states: "For a long while Catholics have made the comment that the 'sola gratia' of the Reformers is 'authentically Christian' and that it is 'in perfect harmony with Catholic tradition, the great conciliar definitions on grace and salvation, and even with Thomism,'" p. 54. See also Karl Rahner, *Theological Investigations,* vol. 1 (Crossroad, N.Y.: Crossroad; London: Darton, Longman & Todd, 1963) and Piet Fransen, *The New Life of Grace* (New York: Desclee; London: Chapman, 1969).

[5]Tom Wright in *The Great Acquittal,* p. 15.

[6]Tony Lane, *The Lion Concise Book of Christian Thought* (Tring, England: Lion, 1984), pp. 219-20; this volume is published in the U.S. as *Harper's Concise Book of Christian Thought* (New York: Harper & Row, 1984).

[7]P. Bläser, quoted in Harding Meyer, *One in Christ,* vol. 17, part 2 (Bedfordshire, England: Turvey Abbey, 1981), p. 104.

[8]Quoted by Harding Meyer in *One in Christ,* vol. 17, part 2, p. 105.

[9]Michael Schmaus, *Dogma Six: Justification and the Last Things* (New York and London: Sheed & Ward, 1977), p. 58.

[10]Meyer, *One in Christ,* vol. 17, part 2, p. 102.

[11]*Decrees of the Council of Trent* 6.16.

[12]For a specialist treatment see B. Bartmann, *Lehrbuch der Dogmatik* (W Germany: Heider Verlag, 1932).

[13]Rahner, *Theological Investigations,* 4: 207.

[14]Meyer, *One in Christ,* vol. 17, part 2, p. 97.

[15]For further development of this subject read H. Chadwick, "Justification by Faith: A Perspective" in *One in Christ* (1984).

[16]See Frederick Grant's response to *Dei verbum* in *Documents of Vatican II,* pp. 129-30. See also Peter Toon, *What's the Difference?* (London: Marshalls, 1983), pp. 51-56.

[17]Josef Geiselmann, *The Meaning of Tradition* (New York: Herder & Herder,

1966).

[18]See the article by R. MacKenzie, S. J., in *Documents of Vatican II,* pp. 107-10.

[19]Lane, *Concise Book of Christian Thought,* p. 216.

[20]*Dei verbum* 1.2.

[21]*Dei verbum* 6.25.

[22]McBrien, *Catholicism,* p. 63.

[23]Ibid., p. 66.

[24]Gerald O'Collins, *Fundamental Theology* (London: Darton, Longman & Todd, 1980; New York: Paulist Press, 1981), p. 236.

[25]The Anglican-Roman Catholic International Commission, *The Final Report* (Windsor: Catholic Truth Society/SPCK, 1982), p. 69.

Chapter 4: Common Reservoir

[1]*The Common Catechism,* edited by Johannes Feiner and Lukas Vischer (New York: Seabury, 1975), is a celebrated and successful attempt by Catholic and Protestant theologians in Germany to offer a joint statement of the Christian faith. The book is divided into five large sections; the first four reveal agreement, while unresolved theological issues are raised in the final section.

[2]Karl Rahner and Paul Imhof, *Ignatius of Loyola* (New York and London: Collins, 1979), p. 20.

[3]John Taylor, *The Go-Between God* (London: SCM, 1972; New York: Oxford Univ. Press, 1979), p. 5.

[4]Leon Suenens, *A New Pentecost?* (London: Darton, Longman & Todd, 1974; New York: Seabury, 1975), p. xiii.

[5]Hans Küng, *The Living Church* (New York and London: Sheed & Ward, 1963).

[6]*Dei verbum* 2.10.

[7]A splendid contemporary book that sets out the history and development of the sacraments from a modern Catholic perspective is Joseph Martos, *Doors to the Sacred* (Garden City, N.Y.: Doubleday; London: SCM, 1981).

[8]See Article 25 of the Church of England's Articles of Religion.

[9]Abbott, *Documents of Vatican II,* p. 104. Also Hans Küng, *The Living Church,* pp. 26-31 and Michael Schmaus, *Dogma Four* (New York and London: Sheed & Ward, 1972), chapter ten.

[10]McBrien, *Catholicism,* pp. 683-86.

[11]Ibid.

[12]This famous phrase is based on Augustine's argument in *De Utilitate Credendi* [The usefulness of belief], Library of Christian Classics, vol. 6 (Philadelphia: Westminster; London: SCM), especially section 14.

[13]McBrien, *Catholicism*, p. 968. See also Avery Dulles's categorization of faith in *The Faith That Does Justice*, ed. John C. Haughey (New York: Paulist Press, 1977), pp. 10-46.

[14]Toon, *What's the Difference?* chapter seven.

[15]In this threefold description of *presence*, I am following, with slight adaptation, the thought of John Macquarrie in *Paths of Spirituality* (New York: Harper & Row; London: SCM, 1972), chapter eight.

[16]See the discussion in Macquarrie, ibid. See also Edward Schillebeeckx, *The Eucharist* (New York and London: Sheed & Ward, 1968). Martos states: "The term *transubstantiation*, once found in every Catholic catechism, is virtually unknown to younger Catholics" *(Doors to the Sacred)*, pp. 292-93.

[17]Schillebeeckx, *The Eucharist*.

[18]See McBrien, *Catholicism*, pp. 765-67.

Chapter 5: The Reservoir of Rome

[1]For a helpful description of Catholicism as seen by a Roman Catholic theologian, see McBrien, *Catholicism*, pp. 1171-86.

[2]For example, von Loewenich, *Modern Catholicism*, chapters one and two.

[3]John Newman, *An Essay on the Development of Christian Doctrine* (New York: Penguin, 1974), p. 240.

[4]Von Loewenich, *Modern Catholicism*, p. 143.

[5]See McSweeney, *Roman Catholicism*, chapter nine.

[6]McBrien, *Catholicism*, pp. 937-40.

[7]John Whale, ed., *The Pope from Poland* (New York and London: Collins, 1981).

[8]Ibid., p. 12.

[9]For further reading see von Loewenich, *Modern Catholicism*, pp. 347-66.

[10]*Lumen gentium* 7.49-50.

[11]For a well-argued case for the communion of saints from an Anglican perspective, see Michael Perham, *The Communion of Saints* (London: Alcuin/SPCK, 1980).

[12]Jaroslav Pelikan, *The Riddle of Roman Catholicism* (New York: Abingdon, 1959; London: Hodder and Stoughton, 1960), p. 87.

[13]Peter Hebblethwaite outlines the problems in *Introducing John Paul II* (New York and London: Collins, 1982), especially chapter nine.

[14]Translation is from Edward Yarnold, S. J., *They Are in Earnest* (New York: State Mutual; Slough, England: St. Paul's Press, 1982), p. 66.

[15]Jean Tillard, *The Bishop of Rome* (Wilmington, Del.: Michael Glazier; London: SPCK, 1983).

[16]Ibid., p. 27.

[17]Quoted ibid., p. 41.

[18]Quoted ibid., p. 190. For a more advanced study of this theme, see Fergus Kerr, O.P., "Vatican I and the Papacy," in *The New Blackfriars*, issues April-September, 1979.

[19]Schillebeeckx, *The Eucharist*, especially pp. 105-7.

Chapter 6: Protestant Wellsprings of Faith

[1]See Toon, *What's the Difference?* chapter one.

[2]G. C. Berkouwer, *The Church* (Grand Rapids, Mich.: Eerdmans, 1976), p. 37. See also von Loewenich, *Modern Catholicism*, chapter nine, "Rome and Reformation."

[3]For a helpful but brief analysis of contemporary evangelicalism see Robert Webber, *Common Roots: A Call to Evangelical Maturity* (Grand Rapids, Mich.: Zondervan, 1978).

[4]*A Compend of Luther's Theology*, ed. H. T. Kerr, Jr. (Philadelphia: Westminster, 1943), p. 173.

[5]*Luther's Theology*, p. 58.

[6]*Decrees of the Council of Trent* 6.7.

[7]*Decree on Ecumenism* 20.

[8]*The Final Report*, p. 13.

[9]*Decrees of the Council of Trent* 22.2.

[10]See also Toon, *What's the Difference?* pp. 95-106.

[11]Attention has already been drawn to O'Collins's important book *Fundamental Theology*. See especially chapters six, seven and ten.

[12]Avery Dulles, S. J., *The Resilient Church* (Garden City, N.Y.: Doubleday, 1977; Dublin, Ireland: Gill and Macmillan, 1978).

[13]*Decrees of the Council of Trent* 6.9.

[14]*Decrees of the Council of Trent* 6.13.

[15]F. Clark, "Grace-experience in the Roman Catholic Tradition," *Journal of Theological Studies* 25 (1974): 352-58.

[16]*Luther's Theology*, p. 135.

[17]See also Webber, *Common Roots*, chapter one.

Chapter 7: All at Sea?

[1]See Peter Nichols, *The Pope's Divisions* (New York: Holt, Rinehart and Winston; London: Faber and Faber, 1981); see also McSweeney, *Roman Catholicism*.

[2]David Edwards, *Religion and Change* (London: Hodder and Stoughton, 1969), chapter four.

[3]Jürgen Moltmann, *The Open Church* (London: SCM, 1978), p. 117.

[4]For example, see Hendrik Hart's article in *Out of Concern for the Church*, ed. James Olthuis (Toronto: Wedge Pub., 1970), chapter two.

[5]McBrien, *Catholicism,* pp. 1173-74 (italics his).

[6]Von Loewenich, *Modern Catholicism,* p. 355.

[7]B. Zylstra, "The Crisis of Our Times and the Evangelical Churches," in Olthuis, *Out of Concern for the Church,* p. 93.

[8]Webber, *Common Roots,* p. 64.

[9]R. Martin-Achard, *A Light to the Gentiles* (Edinburgh: Edinburgh Univ. Press, 1962), p. 75.

[10]Wolfhart Pannenberg, Avery Dulles and Carl Braaten, *Spirit, Faith and Church* (Philadelphia: Westminster Press, 1970), p. 80.

[11]Ibid., p. 84.

[12]Peter Berger, *A Rumor of Angels* (New York: Doubleday, 1969), pp. 1-34.

[13]Jürgen Moltmann, *The Crucified God* (New York: Harper & Row; London: SCM, 1974), chapter one.

[14]Alan Richardson, *Introduction to the Theology of the New Testament* (London: SCM, 1958; New York: Harper, 1959), p. 286.

[15]Moltmann, *Open Church,* p. 84.

[16]Hans Küng, *The Church* (London: Burns and Oates, 1967; Garden City, N.Y.: Doubleday, 1976), p. 365.

[17]A most interesting study of the issue of unity will be found in James Olthuis, *Will All the King's Men* (Toronto: Wedge Pub., 1972).

[18]See also John P. Baker, ed., *Christ's Living Body* (London and Eastbourne: Coverdale, 1973), chapter one.

[19]Richard P. McBrien, *Do We Need the Church?* (New York: Harper & Row; Glasgow: Collins, 1969), pp. 173-77.

[20]William A. Visser 't Hooft, *The Renewal of the Church* (London: SCM, 1956; Philadelphia: Westminster Press, 1957), p. 93.

[21]Quoted in Arthur M. Ramsey and Leon-Joseph Suenens, *The Future of the Christian Church* (New York: Morehouse-Barlow, 1970; London: SCM, 1971), pp. 41-42.

[22]Van Dyk in *Will All the King's Men,* p. 89.

Chapter 8: Harbor in Sight?

[1]Jürgen Moltmann, *The Church in the Power of the Spirit* (New York: Harper & Row; London: SCM, 1977), p. 242.

[2]Lucien Cerfaux, *La Communauté Apostolique* (Paris: n.p., 1956), pp. 13-14.